Lenin Lives!

Reimagining the Russian Revolution
1917–2017

T0159051

Lenin Lives!

Reimagining the Russian Revolution
1917–2017

Philip Cunliffe

Winchester, UK
Washington, USA

First published by Zero Books, 2017

Zero Books is an imprint of John Hunt Publishing Ltd., Laurel House, Station Approach,
Alresford, Hants, SO24 9JH, UK
office1@jhpbooks.net
www.johnhuntpublishing.com
www.zero-books.net

For distributor details and how to order please visit the 'Ordering' section on our website.

Text copyright: Philip Cunliffe 2016

ISBN: 978 1 78535 697 1
978 1 78535 698 8 (ebook)
Library of Congress Control Number: 2017937405

A CIP catalogue record for this book is available from the British Library.

Design: Stuart Davies

Printed and bound by CPI Group (UK) Ltd, Croydon, CR0 4YY, UK

We operate a distinctive and ethical publishing philosophy in all
areas of our business, from our global network of authors to
production and worldwide distribution.

CONTENTS

To my PO653 students

Acknowledgements

When I started teaching Marxism at the University of Kent in the academic year 2012/13, occasionally my students would ask me, "What kind of a Marxist are you?" This book provides an answer to their question: a gonzo Marxist. They have constantly challenged me to come up with new ways of introducing, justifying and refreshing the concepts, theories and ideas that I have taught them. The book is dedicated to them.

This book was also variously inspired by the work of Slavoj Žižek, Richard Ned Lebow, James Heartfield, Richard J. Evans, Ross Wolfe, Loren Goldner, @Damn_Jehu, Peter Frase, Francis Spufford, Chris Cutrone, Reid Kane and Ken Macleod. Inspiration also came from browsing the posts of various Internet chat forum participants, especially those of K-Haderach and Cowd. If all these people agreed with everything or even most things in this book, I know I would have done something wrong. Nonetheless, I hope that if any of them come to read this short book, at least they find it stimulating.

I would also like to thank, in no particular order, Alex Hochuli, George Hoare, Frances O'Leary, Chris Bickerton, Lee Jones, Peter Ramsay, Suke Wolton, Charles Devellennes and Yana Bezirganova who all read earlier versions of the manuscript in part or in full. They all encouraged my gonzo tendency of one. A special thank you to Alex Gourevitch for his help in putting together the counter-factual narrative on the post-war revolution in the US. Needless to say, any errors of fact, interpretation and judgement are all mine, as unfortunately errors cannot be eliminated, even in the realm of the counter-factual.

Chapter I

One Hundred Years that Shook the World

A hundred years since the Russian Revolution that was supposed to have swept capitalism away, global capitalism remains intact and unchallenged. The USSR, that state founded by the Russian Revolution, lies on the ash heap of history. The defeat of the Russian Revolution has put paid to hopes of revolutionary social transformation through the seizure of state power. It has put paid to dreams of a radically better world in which social divisions have been eliminated and all oppression abolished. Its defeat has exposed the futility of humanity seeking to remould society and consciously shape its own destiny.

Yet bizarrely the epic triumph of capitalism has left us with only a limited appreciation of its many benefits and achievements. The marvels of mass consumption are routinely reviled as so much crass materialism. Economic growth and industrialization is seen as polarizing and disruptive of nature. The wondrous synergy of global urbanization is seen as the march of slums and squalor or alternatively, as the extension of suburban existential turpitude. The endless miracles of industrialized agriculture are seen as poisonous and destructive, while continual improvements in communication are seen as alienating and intrusive. The mass migration resulting from improved means of transport is seen as deeply threatening to the wealthiest, most technologically advanced and open societies on the planet. We cower before the prospect of planetary catastrophe and ecological collapse. We are tormented by every new scientific discovery and the possibility of greater control that it engenders. We live in collective dread of the marvels of nuclear power and are morbidly consumed by the fantasy that our own creations might one day come to dominate us when robots take over and computers become self-aware. Given all this, one could be forgiven for wondering whether anything else was defeated with the defeat of the Russian Revolution.

Nostalgia for Futures Past

We also know that once upon a time, the future was supposed to have been better. At the height of the Cold War, people looked forward to a glittering era of peaceful international cooperation, limitless clean energy, populated lunar bases, mass space tourism, colonization of the Solar System, flying cars and robots as domestic servants – and of course, jet packs and hover boards. In the 1959 Kitchen Debate in Moscow, the then US vice president Richard Nixon sparred with Soviet leader Nikita Khrushchev over which social system was capable of delivering not only the best rocket technology but also the best consumer devices. The duels of the Cold War were measured not only by numbers of tanks and missiles, but also by competition over scientific discovery, technical innovation, economic growth, educational advance, urban planning, architecture and even household gadgets – washing machines, toasters, juicers. The Apollo Moon landings, it has been claimed, were the greatest achievements of Soviet communism. If such intense rivalry with the USSR could yield such optimism and hope, should not a capitalist victory over communism have yielded more still? How was it that communism became less threatening, failing to rouse the capitalists to competition?

The states of the old Eastern bloc claimed many lies about themselves – that they were popular, that they were democratic and that they belonged to the people. Yet one lie they never tried to sustain – despite often being ruled by Communist political parties – was that they were communist societies. In his speech delivered to the 22nd Communist Party Congress in 1961, Khrushchev promised communism to the Soviet people by the 1980s. When it became clear that the sputtering Soviet economic engine would never deliver on that promise, Russia's communist leaders never went further than claiming to protect '"actually existing socialism" – a promise whose bad faith was already exposed by the qualifying sobriquet. If communism never happened, and if the hopes of the Russian Revolution fizzled out in Soviet Russia itself long before the Cold War ended, when and where was the Russian Revolution actually defeated? How did communism die?

Capitalist achievements are paltry compared to the scale of capitalist victory. This is so even leaving aside the delusions of no longer existing socialism and the techno-utopianism of the High Cold War. Thirty years since the triumph of liberalism over totalitarianism, and the freest states in the world have chosen to construct industrial scale apparatuses of mass surveillance that would have been the envy of the most efficient secret police of the grimmest People's Republic. Thirty years after the victory of the market over the command economies of the Eastern bloc and the global economy is still struggling to shake off one of its worst ever crises threatening to crumble into a long period of stagnation while global trade collapses and fragments.

Paradoxes abound: the single greatest world-historic achievement of capitalism since the collapse of the USSR – the industrialization of East Asia – has only been attained under the auspices of a ruthless authoritarian state ruled by a murderous Communist Party whose legitimacy is rooted in an autarkic, nationalist revolt against capitalist colonialism. The fate of global capitalism now rests on the ability of a Communist Party to successfully hold down the Chinese workers. As a result of capitalist expansion into Asia, the global production chain for our most advanced technical devices combines astonishing levels of automated production and intellectual achievement with the most primitive forms of resource extraction, the cruellest forms of sweatshop labour and squandering of human potential. Should not the victory of capitalist freedoms over communist totalitarianism have more to show for itself in the annals of human emancipation?

To help answer some of these questions and properly explain some of these historical paradoxes and quirks, I argue that we must ask not only what did happen but also what *could* have happened in the past. This book will go back to 1917 in order to reimagine the Russian Revolution and its results, the better to understand how we have ended up where we are today. Let us begin with a small thought experiment.

A Terrifying Suggestion

Imagine that the natural sciences were to suffer the effects of a catastrophe.[1] Say that an interconnected series of natural disasters, exacerbated by technical failures to respond to them erodes popular belief in science. With science blamed for the crisis and scientists for their failure to respond to it, many scientists are persecuted, assassinated, imprisoned and exiled, while their associates, friends and families fall under suspicion and are targeted for repression. Scientific organizations and institutes are defunded, scientific associations broken up and disbanded. Laboratories are firebombed and closed down, astronomical observatories forsaken on mountaintops. Scientific installations are shuttered, deserted and eventually stripped for spare parts. Scientific institutes will be turned into mosques, eco-lodges and even churches. Laboratories will be transformed into popular museums where visitors are invited to gawp at the ruined instruments of cold, hard rationality and human hubris. Scientific texts are censored and banned in universities, scientists' theories are repressed and purged from teaching, school science teachers are fired from their jobs. Snapping under the pressure or simply swept away by events larger than themselves, many individual scientists renounce science itself as a modern heresy and become among the fiercest critics and persecutors of their former peers, and of science as a body of thought.

Given how deeply science is embedded in modern industrial and technological civilization, the drive to eliminate science would inevitably escalate and heave up all sorts of anachronistic institutions, practices and views in its wake as part of the process of stifling science. Let us further imagine then, that spiralling to greater depths of repression, the drive to counter-science generates Know-Nothing political movements specifically designed to make the process of repression more comprehensive and methodical. Science comes to be seen no longer merely as a set of ideas, theories and practices that anyone can choose to believe and participate in, but as inhering in certain racial minorities and suspect groups that are targeted for systematic mass murder by the Know-Nothings. Know-Nothing dictatorships spread throughout the world, launching invasions to wipe out science in neighbouring states.

Caught up in the maelstrom, science itself begins to fission as scientists and their supporters and allies struggle to respond to these calamities and recuperate from the assaults. Science itself splinters into a range of opposed factions bristling with adjectives embodying their differential responses to the crisis – New Science, Orthodox Science, True Science, Actually Existing Science, Traditional Science and so on. Each group claims to realize the promise of modern science but some of them disguise ever more insidious and murderous forms of counter-science in their attempt to impose monolithic orthodoxy as to what science is and is not. Scientific progress and theoretical development is retarded even further.

After this process has burnt itself out, after the Know-Nothings no longer serve any purpose and have passed into history, and after the internecine science wars have exhausted themselves, science itself is dead. Isolated scientific breakthroughs occur and technological innovation staggers along as in the pre-scientific era, but it remains haphazard, fragmented and poorly understood and theorized, if at all. The eradication of science means that what is left are ruins of scientific devices and laboratories. Knowledge is fragmented, ideas are torn out of theoretical context, and concepts are not only not properly understood but also no longer have any meaningful correspondence to a society that has regressed to a post-scientific era. At a certain point, a new discipline of '"post-science" and "critical science" emerges and even becomes fashionable in certain universities. Here people earnestly discuss Einstein's theory of general relativity alongside alchemical theories of transubstantiation. One theory is as good as the other: neither has any bearing on the natural world because the social world is not configured to incorporate, arbitrate between or advance and institutionalize scientific theory ...

Actually Existing Dystopia

This hypothetical dystopia is, of course, the actually existing social and political world of the twentieth century. Today, people still shrilly denounce "socialism" while others struggle to "reclaim" socialism or insist on their direct inheritance and continuity with the socialist struggles of the past. People still use the words "class", "capitalism", "capital", "working class", "justice", "equality", "oppression", "revolution" and so on, in varying registers and with different polarities but without any real sense of what they mean or stand for. The place occupied by "science" in our earlier hypothetical world is – or rather was – occupied by "scientific socialism" in the actual world. This was the name that German revolutionaries Karl Marx and Friedrich Engels chose to describe their ideas. Scientific socialism was the only coherent doctrine of social change that had mass support while seeking to surpass capitalism *and* build on its achievements. Scientific socialism was – and remains – the only doctrine of post-capitalism that is based on secular modernity, on expanding and deepening the application of science, on accelerating the pace of technological change, on drastically enhancing the rate of economic growth and expansion. It was and remains the only doctrine to combine the ideal of subjugating nature to human will and subjugating the course of human history to human control by abolishing economic exploitation, social hierarchy and by expanding the realm of human self-government through deepening political participation.

Yet if revolutionary communism remains dangerous utopianism or merely idle speculation, we can say with greater certainty that the twentieth century was genuinely dystopian. It is not difficult to see the analogue for the hypothetical wave of counter-science repression sketched out above in our own near past. The actual historical world of the twentieth century saw an unrelenting, rolling global campaign of repression sweep across every continent from the start of the twentieth century through to its bitter end in the 1980s. Working class parties and labour organizations were variously shattered and broken through the use of courts, every conceivable type of police force – regular, secret and private – state repression, assassination and exile and even the use of military force against miners, the unemployed, railway workers, factory workers, dockers, hunger marchers, landless labourers and others. Workers' parties were banned, their leaders imprisoned and their followers persecuted – oftentimes alongside friends, families, allies and associates of every stripe. Civil rights were abused and rescinded, presses and media organizations censored, banned and burned down, individuals blacklisted, fired from their jobs and purged from their professional and industrial associations and unions. All this was only in the richest and freest states of the North Atlantic world. Elsewhere mass murder in the midst of both international and civil war could be the instrument of choice. The Jews of Eastern Europe, the ethnic Chinese of South East Asia, the indigenous peasants of Central America were seen as living physical embodiments of communism that necessitated physical excision from the body of society through programmes of mass extermination.

So fierce was the need to escalate this spiral of oppression that it even became necessary to recreate those very structures of authority, hierarchy and tradition that liberals had once sought to liquidate. Institutions such as the Church, absolutist monarchies, empires, landed interests and latifundism, racial subjugation and women's repression all had to be recreated. Once set upon, such an enormous and violent task of repression could not be contained nor limited. Unsurprisingly it spilled over from anti-communism into an all-out assault on the achievements of modernity itself in which communism was rooted. This required dispersing the very notion of a common humanity without which ideas of democracy, equality and freedom are meaningless – a feat accomplished through notions of racial hierarchy and cultural segmentation. After all, the only coherence to the absurd morass of fascist ideologies and movements that swept throughout Europe, Asia and the Americas was the violent and authoritarian anti-communism at their core.

All this is without even treating of the efforts to suppress revolution in the name of socialism itself. Here there was not only the grotesque show trials of Russia's revolutionary leadership in the 1930s, but also the indiscriminate purges that annihilated an entire generation of socialist political leaders and organizers throughout Europe via Stalin's usurpation of the Comintern, the international revolutionary organization established in 1919. In his remembrance of the Spanish Civil War, George Orwell recalls that in revolutionary Barcelona in 1936 it was more dangerous to appear dressed as a worker than as a member of the middle classes, as Stalin's death squads patrolled the city in a murderous rampage against left wing dissent.[2]

The only way to properly contextualise and understand this tangled skein of violent struggle, political oppression and social retardation is through locating it in the dialectic of revolution and counter-revolution at the global level. It is then that we can bring into focus the colossal scale of the violence, reaction and oppression that was necessary to arrest social evolution and progress. In that process the social and political basis for progress was destroyed – oftentimes literally, in mass murder. Across the world, those social forces and political movements who had the incentive and will to overcome established hierarchies of race, class and gender and inherited privilege, and to liquidate traditional structures of oppression and control, were variously destroyed, mangled, contained or diverted. The result is worse than a world without science, for what we are left with is an alienated world that is incapable of reconciling itself to science and unlocking the still untapped potential of science to reshape society. Progress existed before science – how else could the Scientific Revolution ever have come about? – and now science has been condemned to outlive social and political progress. What this means is that we live in the aftermath of dystopia. The mid-twentieth century was the catastrophic nadir of human history and we stand on the other side, even though it remains in living memory.

The defeat of revolutionary communism, the defeat of the left and the mangling of the global labour movements and its allies is a truism – even if it is only weakly accepted and more weakly understood. As theorist of the New Left Perry Anderson observes, "For the first time since the Reformation, there are no longer any significant oppositions – that is, systematic rival outlooks – within the thought world of the West; and scarcely any on a world scale either, if we discount religious doctrines as largely inoperative archaisms".[3] Understanding this is vital to a proper understanding of society and politics at the global level.

The political right, so long defined by its opposition to communism, remains incapable of accepting its world-historic victory in the Cold War. Thirty years since the collapse of the USSR and the political right is still convulsed by Red panics, hysterically proclaiming the extent of socialist infiltration and the need to reclaim their countries. Isolated, tenured mandarins of critical theory and postmodernism are blamed for having single-handedly overturned Western civilization by infiltrating the academy with gnostic teachings that they themselves only dimly comprehend. Frumpy social democrats such as Jeremy Corbyn in Britain and Bernie Sanders in the US, shambolic left populist parties such as Syriza in Greece and Podemos in Spain are decried as fanatical and ruthless communists in the financial pages. Mild policies of gentle redistribution and modest public sector expansion are denounced as threatening immediate economic ruination. With labour militancy and rates of unionization at historic lows in the advanced economies, even isolated episodes of workplace conflict are routinely inflated into the prospect of anarchic social collapse: "the watchword constantly recurs, the theme remains always the same, the verdict is ever ready and invariably reads: 'Socialism'". Over 150 years later Karl Marx's diagnosis of conservative hysteria in mid-nineteenth-century France still rings true today: "Even bourgeois liberalism is declared socialistic, bourgeois enlightenment socialistic, bourgeois financial reform socialistic ..."[4]

Wars and Class Wars

If the Right is incapable of realizing that it won, the Left is incapable of realizing how they lost. Under the influence of martial metaphors devised by Stalin's Italian henchman, Antonio Gramsci, the left today still has difficulty properly conceiving of the nature of its defeat. Gramsci concocted his theories in fascist prison, shortly after he led the Italian revolution to defeat in the aftermath of the Great War. Using metaphors drawn from the preceding war, Gramsci conceived of social and political struggle as being of essentially two types. There was the "war of manoeuvre" – an out and out assault on the state as with the Bolshevik storming of the Winter Palace in 1917 – and a "war of position", the latter being more akin to trench warfare, except that this took place by seizing "hegemony" over the institutions of civil society.

Still gripped by imagery taken from a total war that happened a century ago, the left has tended to think of political and social struggle as a set piece affair that happens across discrete periods of time like an actual military battle on some imagined field removed from society. As everyone knows about trench warfare, no one advances very far very fast. Defeat only means that the metaphorical battle lines shift a little, and the enemy captures a few more inches of useless territory. Such warfare is even less threatening when the trenches turn out to be so comfortable, as the tenured academic left has discovered. As a result Gramsci's successors have lost sight of the fact that in social and political struggle, society is not a location that is somehow separate from the field of battle. Rather society itself is constituted through the struggles and schisms that structure it. Defeat is thus not a matter of having lost metaphorical ground elsewhere, but has instead resulted in the reorganization of society itself around the defeat of the left and the suppression of communism.

Many leftists still talk as if the struggle continues, usually at a conveniently safe distance from the lecture hall, such as in Palestine, Venezuela or Rojava. Yet it is the defeat of the party of movement, the defeat of the social and political forces of progress, which explains core features of contemporary society. It is class defeat that helps explain the political decay and fragmentation of liberal societies. Less than thirty years after the vindication of capitalist democracy over communist totalitarianism, the democratic structures and institutions of Western society are crumbling at a startling pace as traditional mass political parties dissipate and powerful anti-political trends of apathy, populism and anti-corruption intersect and reinforce each other. Once it is understood that the defeat of communism required disabling institutions of mass political participation, then the fact that political systems of the West are still being dragged down by the sinking of the USSR becomes less mysterious.

It is the defeat of communism that explains how liberal societies constituted by reference to individual freedom have inherited and continue to recreate vast infrastructures of state oppression and control. It is class struggle and defeat that explains why these societies maintain legal systems lacerated by a plethora of draconian provisions stemming from workplace clashes, strikes, world wars, cold wars, labour control, anti-colonial wars and domestic states of emergency. It helps explain how the US remains the most militarized liberal society in history, having constructed global imperial structures justified by anti-communism that the US political system is now incapable of liquidating. It is class struggle and defeat that explains how a liberal society can imprison more of its own people than today's most ruthless authoritarian states, and operate such a viciously punitive and barbaric penal system. Not least it is defeat that helps explain the generalized malaise and hostility to progress, as the next stage of human development vanished from view and the future was folded into an endless present.

It is defeat that explains the most peculiar paradox of all – that the suppression of communism *entailed the suppression of capitalism itself*. As a social system propelled by social struggles between economic groups more than it is a system defined by market competition, it was inevitable that a shift in the balance of forces between these groups would impact the social system itself. It is defeat and the shattering of unions that helps explain the sinking of the richest countries in the world into low inflation economies with stagnating real wages. It is defeat that helps explain the fragmented and tiered labour markets of Europe that set groups of workers against each other. It is defeat that helps explain the decline of productivity growth, the failure to harness new technologies for economic growth and progress, and wilting rates of business investment.

Strange Defeat?

It seems a strange proposition that defeat could explain the existing order of society. It would seem an even stranger proposition to reconcile with Karl Marx's ideas, associated as they are with deterministic accounts of social change and historic development that roused their followers with visions of a radiant and inevitable communist utopia. Yet the prospect of defeat was built into the assumptions of Marxian communism from the start. In the *Communist Manifesto* with which Karl Marx and Friedrich Engels proclaimed their political ideas publicly and systematically for the first time, they reckoned with the prospect that the class struggle – by its very nature *as* struggle – might end in defeat. They called this the "common ruin of the contending classes". Instead of seeing human development as the victory of one side over another in a geopolitical stand-off, they envisaged the future as the prospect of revolutionary, internal renewal in the most advanced societies – in capitalism itself. If social struggle could not be resolved so as to ratchet human development onto the next level, then that failure was not just a defeat for those challenging the existing order but a collective defeat for humanity as such as it stymied progress. Thus defeat was ultimately a defeat for the defenders of the status quo too, as the status quo decayed into historical quagmire.

In all likelihood Marx and Engels had ancient Rome in mind when they considered this prospect. They looked back to how the social struggles of the early Roman Republic were resolved by the collapse into monarchical empire – this despite the Republic being a state founded on the express rejection of monarchy. It is a significantly different view of Roman decline from the conventional one. Instead of beginning with the downward slope from unified monarchical empire into barbarian fragments, decline begins with the upward thrust to imperial splendour. Thus the end of progress is not the collapse into the Gothic kingdoms as with the fall of the Western Empire in 476 CE, but is rather embodied in the perpetual frontier wars and bread and circuses that preceded it.[5] It is a striking and chilling proposition: "common ruin" need not mean the implosion of social order and state power. Ruin can be prolonged and disguised, perhaps even for a millennium. Moreover this outcome has to be explained by reckoning with an earlier defeat not on a battlefield between legionnaires and barbarians, but in an internal social struggle between plebeians and patricians. Such a view gives us a new perspective on seeing Marxism as a doctrine of inevitability – and perhaps one closer to Marx's own original vision. Beyond the demands imposed by propaganda to rally and rouse support, Marx claimed not so much that communism was inevitable but that it was necessary – that it was a resolution to the contradictions of capitalist society. Necessity imposes stringent demands but what is necessary is by no means inevitable.

Marx's gushing praise for capitalism famously exceeds anything that could be found in the pages of the *Financial Times*, the *Wall Street Journal* or the *Economist* even today – let alone in the defence offered of the market in the nineteenth century. Marx is even more specific, lavishing praise on the bourgeoisie itself, which "has been the first to show what man's activity can bring about. It has accomplished wonders far surpassing Egyptian pyramids, Roman aqueducts, and Gothic cathedrals; it has conducted expeditions that put in the shade all former Exoduses of nations and crusades."[6] Not only did Marx admire the tremendous productiveness and wealth generated by capitalism, he also admired it precisely for those aspects of market society that still fills defenders of the market with dread: its dissolution of all inherited institutions, traditions and authorities, notably those of state, nation, kinship and religion. While liberals, anarchists and others sought to overthrow churches and kings, Marx grasped that subversion was already itself the mode of authority in capitalism, that capitalism institutionalized transgression as orthodoxy:

Constant revolutionizing of production, uninterrupted distur-
bance of all social conditions, everlasting uncertainty and
agitation distinguish the bourgeois epoch from all earlier
ones. All fixed, fast-frozen relations, with their train of ancient
and venerable prejudices and opinions, are swept away, all
new-formed ones become antiquated before they can ossify.
All that is solid melts into air, all that is holy is profaned, and
man is at last compelled to face with sober senses his real
conditions of life, and his relations with his kind.[7]

As Marx's own example shows, only true communists can truly
appreciate capitalism. Marx, cast for so long as the demonic
theorist of political upheaval and bloody tumult, envisaged
socialist revolution less to disrupt as much as to consciously steer
a society already riven by disruption.

Thus neither Marx nor Engels envisaged communism as "a
state of affairs which is to be established, an ideal to which reality
[will] have to adjust itself. We call communism the real
movement which abolishes the present state of things ..."[8] Thus
communism was not the property of revolutionary conspirators
subverting established authority or imposing their visions of
reform and change, but rather had to express the dynamic of
capitalism pushing past itself, of which the revolutionary
conspirators were the expression – and oftentimes the uncon-
scious expression. Marx swiped at the insurrectionists and
conspirators of his era such as Louis Blanqui, Pierre-Joseph
Proudhon and Mikhail Bakunin, whose followers furiously
battled the *ancien regime* on the barricades while languishing in
the shadow of the new factories. Nineteenth-century revolutionaries declaimed for nation and liberty while dreaming of ancient
Sparta and Rome, unaware that far greater and unprecedented
revolutionary forces were at work in the factories of England and
expanding circuits of global trade. While even liberals understood that capitalism was revolutionary and subversive of the old

order, of pre-modern societies and European absolutism, Marx went further in seeing that capitalism was revolutionary and subversive *of itself* – and that this opened the possibility of remaking society entirely.

Suppressing communism did not mean therefore merely rooting out conspirators and locking up subversives, launching anti-guerrilla sweeps through mountains and jungles or building geopolitical alliances and mass producing tanks and rockets to deter foreign enemies ... repressing communism necessitated nothing less than arresting the course of human development itself. If this contention is right that we live in a society which has been organized around defeat, then it is not idle speculation but absolutely necessary to understand what could have happened – what were the stakes of this social struggle?

It's the political economy, stupid

In as much as Marx and Engels have had any impact on social science and history, it is to be cast as economic determinists. In this schema, it is the struggle over material resources between social groups that is the dynamic of society, and all social and political claims can be decoded in terms of underlying economic interests. In short, there is limited scope for the exercise of conscious human will and choice in shaping society. Plenty of ink has been spilled in efforts logically to resolve and finesse Marx's notorious architectural metaphor of "base" and "superstructure" in describing the relationship between the economy and the rest of society. Used infrequently across many publications and writings, the entirety of Marx's work is reduced to the banal insight that resonates so effectively with contemporary cynicism and platitudes about globalization ... "it's the economy, stupid": big business buys off politicians, bankers get paid more than ordinary workers, etc., etc.

To take this line would be to reckon without the philosophical background to Marx's work, and to ignore his core analysis of political economy. Marx took the critique of religion developed by early nineteenth-century German philosophers and generalized it across society. Just as the supernatural attributes of the religious world could be decoded in terms of their origins in human needs, ideas and aspirations, so too Marx claimed, could society itself. As we were ruled in religion by the creation of our minds, so we were ruled in market society by the creation of our own hands. Moreover expanding the realm of conscious human control and awareness required not merely dispelling superstition but a transformation of the society itself that persistently generated such illusion and deception. In other words, it was less that Marx decoded society in terms of material things and resources, but rather that he decoded material things and economic forces in terms of human agency: the "stuff" of society was the outcome of human choice and will, society itself malleable and subject to human choice. If society itself is malleable, then the issue becomes whether or not that choice is willed or not, conscious or not.

Marx's view of human collective human choice was therefore not to trivialize it but to give it potentially greater scope: at certain junctures and under certain specific conditions, there was the possibility to alter the pattern of human development. Class struggle was not merely the tugging back and forth of economic self-interest between different groups, but also had historic dimensions, raising the prospect of conscious choice on an historic and not merely individual or collective level. In the words of German revolutionary Rosa Luxembourg the ' "task" of revolutionary socialism was "the conquest of political power": "This conception of our task is closely related to our conception of capitalist society ... our view that capitalist society is caught in insoluble contradictions which will ultimately necessitate an explosion, a collapse, at which point we will play the role of the banker-lawyer who liquidates a bankrupt company."[9] No one understood this task better than the leader of the majority faction of the Russian Social Democrats, Vladimir Lenin.

Reimagining History the Right Way ...

Counterfactual or virtual history is often seen as the preserve of the Right – of conservative and military historians, the kind of people who might like to dress up in grey uniforms on the weekend and wistfully re-enact the Battle of Gettysburg, or pore over the decisions of Great Men and grub about in their personal psychology. The overwhelming focus of existing counterfactual and alternative history covers three basic scenarios: (1) Nazi victory in the Second World War, with all the details of Nazi triumph lasciviously imagined in the tiniest detail; (2) Confederate victory in the US civil war, and (3) scratching World War I from the historical record. All three underscore the rightist bias of "virtual history". Such reimaginings cut against modern historiography, focused either on the irreversible momentum of social and economic change, or else caught up in the shimmering flux of cultural and sociological patterns of identity creation and recreation. Political decisions by leaders at key junctures dissolve into the ether.

What is striking about the usual domains of counterfactual history is how poorly they can accommodate these exercises in historical reimagination. The simplest way to see the inevitable outcomes of Confederate and Nazi defeats, for example, is simply to look at the statistics showing us the industrial resources available to each side in those respective conflicts. This does not mean that political choices had no role to play in conflicts that were nonetheless essentially attritional. As Evan Mawdsley makes clear in his history of the Eastern Front, given the significant material superiority of the British Empire and USSR over Nazi Germany – let alone when combined with that of the USA – the issue is less why did the war end the way it did but rather why did it take *so long* to end the way it did.[10] It is a question made all the more poignant by the fact that so much of the war's death and destruction, including the final eclipse of European Jewry, came in its closing stages across 1943–45.

Even this manoeuvre – simply to read the outcome of the war off the balance of industrial production and manpower – would still miss a crucial underlying issue. To ask what if Hitler had done this or that differently – what if he had invested more resources in the Nazi A-bomb? or jet fighters? or ballistic rockets? or timed his invasion to avoid the Russian winter? – is to misconceive the fundamental character of the Nazi project.[11] Contrary to the impression of ruthless totalitarian efficiency, the Nazis were incapable of sovereign decision-making and therefore incapable of the effective, rational allocation of resources. The very profusion of secret "wonder weapons" speaks to the Nazis' inability to make decisive, strategic choices. Indeed, the Nazis expressly organized themselves to function in this way, not least in sanctifying individual caprice as enshrined in the fascist "Leader Principle".[12] This insight of modern historiography into the chaotic dynamics of Nazi politics is itself a rediscovery of theories devised by German Marxists of the Weimar period who, unlike the many liberals who criticized totalitarianism, were never secretly enthralled by the prospect of men in uniforms and jackboots ordering them about.[13]

The point therefore, is that there is no reason to accept counterfactual history as the natural home or exclusive monopoly of military and conservative historiography. Nor should we allow ourselves to get trapped in simplistic, binary accounts of human choice: human agency clearly matters, even when the ultimate outcome is not in doubt, as we saw with the question regarding the duration of the Second World War. *How* human choices matter depends on what level of analysis we are talking about: is it a matter of accelerating or retarding powerful underlying trends propelling the thrust of events, or is it a matter of reconfiguring the very social matrix in which people make their choices to begin with? We must think through how counterfactualism can be done in a way that keys into genuine moments of historical possibility, combined with the instruments consciously to shape the flow of events –appropriate and effective forms of political structure, organization and leadership, apposite political ideals, and appropriate theories of social action and change, as well as a fluid context in which an existing order is being reconfigured. Such a moment existed throughout Europe and America, I argue, in the revolutionary aftermath of the First World War. More than this, there are historical moments that are themselves *self-consciously predicated* on counterfactuals; such was the debate that gripped the Bolshevik Party on the eve of their seizure of power in autumn 1917.

That said, plotting counterfactual outcomes in class wars is a more difficult and delicate exercise than doing the same in inter-state wars. In reimagining the class war we are unable to read the outcome off output statistics measuring national power and strength, as by definition in periods of revolutionary upheaval, that class on whom national power depends – the workers – are withdrawing their political support from the existing order. How then can we be confident about plotting such alternative scenarios?

Rules for Building (Virtual) Socialism

Even if we avoid the usual domains of counterfactual history that require such gross distortions to historical possibility as the masochistic fantasies of Nazi victory, we are still left with the problem of knowing how to do counterfactual history less gratuitously. The dilemma is akin to that in the board game *Jenga*. The aim of the game is continually to withdraw blocks from the structure, which allows it to be extended. Yet the process itself continuously runs the risk of the whole thing collapsing into rubble. If a given historical fact or event is analogous to the wooden blocks from the board game, how can we know in advance whether withdrawing it from the historical sequence would lead the whole structure to conceptual collapse, particularly given that we cannot observe the literal collapse of a given historical sequence of events? Perhaps a more precise analogy would be to a higher level version of *Jenga* in which the tower itself not only runs the risk of collapse as blocks are withdrawn, but also spontaneously reassembles *itself* in response to the strategic removal of certain blocks. We remain with the basic problem of counterfactual history: given how hard it is to establish what actually *did* happen, why complicate things by speculating on what *might* have happened, and run the risk of collapsing an historical sequence that at least has the benefit of having *actually* happened?

Given how much social science and history is at least implicitly predicated on counterfactuals, fortunately there have been scholarly efforts to sharpen the tools and procedures needed for such analysis. Moreover, as we have seen with Russian revolutionary history, sometimes counterfactualism is not merely a speculative add-on to the historical process but absolutely integral to understanding the actual historical process itself. How adroitly I manage to play this historical game of *Jenga*, to withdraw and reposition historical blocks in the following chapters, and whether or not I manage to avoid it all collapsing into rubble, is left to the reader to judge. At the very least, I hope that the withdrawal of blocks from the structure provides new perspective and insight on what's left: how does it all look when key historical episodes such as the Second World War, fascism, Stalinism, the Third World are removed from the tower? That is to say, I hope at the very least that the intellectual exercise of imaginatively altering the past, even if unconvincing in part or even in whole, helps us better understand what did happen and why it might have happened the way it did.

In what follows, we begin by considering how Marxists confronted the historical choices given to them at the time of the

Russian Revolution. The chapter after that presents the counter-factual narrative of the globalizing revolution – counter-factual as in, "contrary to the facts". The 1920s was a period of revolutionary upheaval and tumult around the world, but ultimately the revolution failed to spread from Russia. In chapter three, key facts and details are changed around a new story of historical and revolutionary change. A historical narrative is offered, presenting in broad brush strokes the spread of revolution around the developed world in the 1920s. In this third chapter, the 1920s is portrayed as a revolutionary period like the 1950s in the Third World of our era, or the late eighteenth to early nineteenth centuries in the Atlantic world, or the Arab Spring in the Middle East of today. Unlike these other examples, this revolutionary convulsion happens in the developed core of the global economy – something not seen since the late 1840s in Europe. Chapter three is the single longest chapter in this book, as this counter-factual narrative is interwoven with actual historical facts and details so that the points of contrast between actuality and reality are sharply expressed. The counterfactual narrative thus switches back and forth with the history of our actually existent world. I refer to the actual history of the twentieth century as "the historical world" in order to differentiate it from the counter-factual timeline discussed in this book.

Historical forces, social change and economic imperatives are ultimately only expressed through the lives of individuals, so the fourth chapter tries to do this, by recounting how the lives of many people may have been different as a result. This is done again in broad brush strokes. It is expressly designed to be indicative, demonstrative and provocative rather than exhaustive or comprehensive. A cross-section of different domains (art, science, politics, etc.) is discussed by way of providing some holistic perspective. Of course, if some key facts are altered, it begs the question of why not alter all the others too? In this book, I hew as closely as possible to the lives of actual historical figures in order to more closely track the differences in lived historical changes in a counter-factual world. Obviously, the detail of individuals' lives are far more contingent than altering the scope of broad historic forces, but talking about a caste of individuals that is familiar to our actual, historical world serves a narrative purpose here in helping to concretize how life might have been different in an altered timeline.

Marxism was the grandest of grand narratives, and the grandest project of human emancipation. It aimed to expand human freedom from political emancipation to social emancipation, not only eradicating despotism but also ending the oppression of labour in civil society, and in so doing overturning both state and civil society itself. The failure of Marxism should be of interest to anyone concerned in human freedom and its future. So how did Marxists used to see the future of human freedom?

Chapter Two

Possible Worlds: Socialism or Barbarism

It is an unseasonably warm November 2017 in Leningrad, although within planned temperature ranges. There is discussion among atmospheric engineers and climate planners whether to make minor adjustments to the cloud systems they are responsible for in order to reflect more sunlight away from the northern hemisphere, or whether to accelerate the construction of orbiting Lagrange space mirrors intended for longer term climate control. Without such geoengineering, the planet would be even warmer. Such is the result of 90 years of unbroken, rapid global economic growth and the industrialization of Asia and Africa. It is precisely this global development that provides the requisite levels of wealth, technological advance and engineering nous to conceive and mount such significant and ambitious efforts at climate control. By the same token, high levels of global wealth and more widely and generously distributed levels of industrial abundance have facilitated the dissolution of rigid state structures, competing power centres and international hierarchies that would otherwise make the collective coordination necessary for climate control on a planetary scale so much more fraught and difficult.

In Leningrad itself, a modest new statue of Russian revolutionary leader Vladimir Ilich Lenin is unveiled, alongside a new novelty bar that opens in the same square and boasts solid gold urinals in order to fulfil one of Lenin's less well-known predictions. There are a handful of such statues scattered across Eurasia, implicitly abiding by Lenin's remark that statues were better suited to pigeon shit than humans. Elsewhere, a newly minted spaceship is named *The Dreamer in the Kremlin* in Lenin's honour. Intended to carry supplies to colonists on the Red Planet, the craft is named after the title of an interview that Lenin gave to the great British science fiction author H.G. Wells nearly a century earlier, in which Lenin stunned Wells when he proclaimed his intent to introduce a national electricity grid throughout Russia before even Britain had one. The dynamism and optimism of revolution has provided plenty of inspiration for blessing humanity's solar expansion. Irish revolutionary James Connelly's slogan adorns the ageing orbiting agricultural laboratory *Stars and Plough*, while the ship *Storming the Heavens* that is carrying explorers to the moons of Jupiter – king of the gods in the pantheon of the ancients – is inspired by the slogans of German communist Karl Liebknecht. Back in Leningrad, some revellers wake up with sore heads the next morning after partying in the bars around Nevsky Prospekt: gold is put to good use in the new bar. Otherwise celebrations of the centenary are fairly low key. There are more significant centenaries to celebrate in the coming years, such as the spread of the revolution from Russia to what was – back then at least – the industrialized core of the world in Western Europe and the US. These later struggles threw up a generation of revolutionary leaders whose successes overshadowed those of Lenin and his Bolsheviks.

That aside, this is a world in which people are more accustomed to looking forward than backwards. Nor are there any particular interests that need to be serviced through orchestrated public commemorations of historical events. Historical retrospection is further overwhelmed by collective discussion of the strange signals emanating from a peculiar and distant star 1,480 light years away named KIC8462852. So unusual is the pattern of erratic flickering emitted by this star that astronomers have no choice but to be forced to reckon with even the most outlandish hypotheses – such as the possibility that the irregular dimming might be caused by a swarm of artificial alien structures designed to capture the majority of the star's emitted energy. Even when this possible explanation is excluded, the star's dimming cannot be convincingly explained by any known natural phenomena. Spurred by this mystery, global discussion persists as to when to begin galactic expansion in order to investigate extra-solar planetary systems properly.

Controversy rages: on the one hand, there are the neo-cosmists, insisting that humanity cannot rest content with anything as insular as socialism in one solar system and that resources and effort must be devoted to exploration of extra-solar planetary systems. On the other hand, there are the solists, who claim that there is more than enough adventure, discovery and resources to occupy humanity for many years yet among the inner planets, the Jovian and Saturnian moons and the asteroid belt. Many of the solists urge that humanity accelerate its collective energy consumption so that we reach Type II on the Kardashev scale. Or in other words, that we construct a system-sized solar array that would be able to capture much more of the energy radiated by our sun, so that we too would appear like star KIC8462852 to aliens looking at us from a distance of 1,000 light years away. Yet for all the energy and passion and heated faction-alism, it is not a political struggle invoking the seizure of power and defeat of opposition, as there is no state to command, or institutions to capture, no commanding heights of the economy to conquer, no material interests represented in the debate between the various sides. Planetary resources are so abundant that whatever option is chosen will not compromise anyone's standard of life. Instead, it is that rare thing – a genuine disagreement. Society has become a pure technocracy, in which administration no longer requires people to be treated as things.

Of Starlight and Progress

Back in our 2017, star KIC8462852 remains entirely real and – at the time of writing at least – still mysterious. Our actually existing astronomers have had to take hypotheses from science fiction in trying to eliminate possible explanations for the strange signals emitted by KIC8462852. Otherwise KIC8462852 shines on a very different world from the one described at the start of this chapter. Whatever explains its erratic shining, the only thing that we know for certain is that given the distance it took that starlight to travel to us, whatever happened to star KIC8462852 happened deep in the past. When the dimming that we are only now witnessing actually occurred about 1,480 years ago, Byzantine emperor Justinian was struggling to reunite the Roman Empire, his generals only having recently reconquered North Africa and Italy from the barbarians. His basilica, the Hagia Sophia, will remain the largest cathedral in the world for a thousand years hence, and an architectural marvel given the Romans' inability to manufacture steel beams and girders. Justinian's law code will form the basis for modern Western legal systems hundreds of years later, as well as providing the basis for autonomous universities as centres of learning.

Further east, the recently crowned Anushiruwan the Just will lead the Sasanian Persian Empire to its peak. Despite being embroiled in an endless war with the Byzantines, Anushiruwan will boost the empire through an extensive programme of bridge- and dam-building and through the consolidation of trade routes. He will also strengthen Persia intellectually, in welcoming the philosopher-refugees fleeing Christian fanaticism after Justinian closes down Plato's Academy in Athens. Thus Anushiruwan helped preserve the gains of neoplatonic philosophy for posterity. So how might we measure how far humanity has travelled in the time that it took the erratic starlight of KIC8462852 to reach us? For that matter how might we gauge the further distance to travel between our world of 2017 and the world of 2017 described at the start of this chapter? Or alternatively, how much further might we have been able to progress in the time that it took that starlight to reach Earth?

Despite the length of time it took for light from KIC8462852 to reach us, there have been no significant changes since the days of

Anushiruwan and Justinian. This is true at least according to the Kardashev scale mentioned above. Devised in the early 1960s by Soviet astronomer Nikolai Kardashev, the scale was devised as a way of using known physical and cosmic laws in order objectively to measure technological and civilizational sophistication, including that of any advanced alien species were we ever to encounter them. Kardashev's system does this by tracking the tell-tale cosmic signatures of different levels of energy consumption that are necessary to sustain technologically advanced life-forms. The Kardashev scale itself is divided into three, ranging from planetary to solar to galactic levels of energy consumption. Over the last year at the time of writing, astronomers had implicit recourse to the Kardashev scale when they were forced to rule out the possibility of alien artefacts being responsible for the unprecedented dimming of KIC8462852.

According to US physicist Michio Kaku, at our current level of early twenty-first-century development, we are perhaps one to two centuries away from Type I levels of energy consumption.[1] It is probably not an accident that it was a Soviet astronomer who devised this scale in the first place. It is such a fundamental premise of Marxism that human history progresses through stages that this basic notion of civilizational advance could survive even through the distortions wreaked upon Marxist theory by Soviet officialdom. Such notions had to be retained as they were vital to the Soviet justification of the USSR as a superior society to the West, the USSR embodying the next stage of human progress.

Yet Marx and Engels' grand schema of human development is at once more simple and more complicated than the Kardashev scale. It is more complicated in that it focuses on the internal architecture of changing complexes of property relations and technology, whose significant differences might never outwardly manifest themselves in anything as obvious as heat emitted as a by-product of total energy consumption. As Marx puts it in his study of political economy:

> The specific economic form, in which unpaid surplus-labour
> is pumped out of direct producers, determines the
> relationship of rulers and ruled, as it grows directly out of
> production itself ... It is always the direct relationship of the
> owners of the conditions of production to the direct producers
> – a relation always naturally corresponding to a definite stage
> of the methods of labour and thereby its social productivity –
> which reveals the innermost secret, the hidden basis of the
> entire social structure, and with it the political form of the
> relation of sovereignty and dependence, in short, the corre-
> sponding specific form of the state.[2]

Any number of variations on how surplus labour is extracted
from direct producers would all still fall into what we might call
a "Type 0", or pre-planetary Kardashev civilization, at least as
measured by total energy consumption. This would be
irrespective of whether the owner of the "conditions of
production" was – to take some of Marx's examples – an
"Athenian aristocrat, an Etruscan theocrat, a Roman citizen, a
Norman baron, an American slave-owner, a Wallachian boyar, a
modern landlord or a capitalist".[3]

Despite then offering us more finely polished lenses to
measure civilizational advance and social evolution, in another
sense the Marxian schema is also simpler than the Kardashev
scale. For Marx and Engels provided only the barest sketches of
what the next, more advanced stages of human civilization might
look like, without recourse to projecting growth in crude
aggregate quantities such as total global energy consumption.
Nor, for that matter, did either of them ever express any longing
to look down from giant placards onto the May Day military
parades in Red Square that were annual occurrences in
Kardashev's day. As mid-nineteenth-century German commu-

nists, Marx and Engels saw the future as lying in upgrading the rich, industrial west rather than merely boosting the poor, rural east. Beyond extrapolating geometric growth in such gross measures of civilizational progress as total energy production, peering into a parallel, more futuristic present is thus necessarily speculative on plenty of details. Moreover Marx and Engels notoriously took a dim view of such speculative efforts. They self-consciously constructed their own ideas in direct opposition to those they criticized as "utopian socialists" who were absorbed with designing intricate blueprints for the future in ever more baroque and complex forms right down to, in the case of Charles Fourier, regulating the timing and frequency of sexual inter-course. Both Marx and Engels steadfastly refused to describe in any significant detail the communist future for which they aimed, and generally avoided giving any positive content to their vision. So where does that leave us?

Socialism: Utopian, Scientific and Virtual

Marx and Engels' rejection of utopia-mongering was not out of intellectual obstinacy or laziness. Nor was it an exercise in political evasion. On the contrary, it was fully reasoned and publicly justified. It is worth examining these reasons a little more closely to see how far they still stand up, and how they relate to the discussion in this book. Marx, so often charged with being an obstinate utopian determined to fit humanity into his procrustean bed without regard to the foibles of human nature, was in fact the original and most consistent critic of utopian thinking – not least because he was able to see its power and appeal. Marx and Engels' refusal to provide details of communism spoke to their understanding of social change and their democratic instincts. Given the extent to which ideas are shaped by the context in which they emerge, whatever the present had to say about the future would inevitably always end up saying more about ourselves than it would about the future.

Worse, such prognoses might simply degenerate into ideological fantasy. In any case, even if we were capable of greater certainties about the future, why should the present impose its own priorities, preconceptions and prejudices onto a more advanced society?

Nor was Marx and Engels' hostility to utopianism uniform. They had tremendous respect for those they described as the utopian socialists – a caste of Anglo-French visionaries and reformers of the late eighteenth and early nineteenth centuries. Among the greatest of these was the Comte de Saint-Simon, a French aristocrat who renounced his title and bequeathed to Marxism the ideas of industrial revolution, of social development being driven by changing forms of property ownership and the development of the productive system, of productive classes as opposed to idle ruling classes, and a vision of the future in which centralized structures of political coercion and control would dissolve into spontaneous social self-organization – a vision in which the "administration of things" would replace the "government of man". Where Marx and Engels criticized Saint-Simon and other utopian socialists was for being apolitical. These were essentially civil society movements based on withdrawal into communistic colonies in the New World, hoping to spread their ideals through education, reform and example. Such limited means of dissemination belied the grandness of their visions, and reflected their absence of any theory of social change.

Incapable of identifying any specific social group with the interest and incentive to mount such social transformation, they were often reduced to pleading with the powers that be: Saint-Simon mounted appeals to both Napoleon and the latter's great rival, Tsar Alexander I. Saint-Simon's followers would eventually evolve into a weird secular cult that would glorify and idolize capitalist entrepreneurs, visionary engineers and buccaneering industrialists. In contrast to this degeneration, it was the identification of a social group that was capable of carrying social transformation through in line with wider social changes that Marx and Engels considered their advance on the utopian socialists. This group was the proletariat: people whose property was in themselves and their labour-power, and who had to work for wages to live. From Marx and Engels' point of view, propelling the efforts of the proletariat to emancipate itself in the here and now made speculations about the future even more redundant.

The dearth of utopianism of today and the subsequent enervation of culture and politics have been widely remarked upon. The place once occupied by the utopian socialists is today occupied – sometimes literally – by a morass of sub-anarchistic and ecological groups. These groups share many of the defects of the utopian socialists on top of which they have added plenty of their own. At the same time, they fail to compensate for these flaws, as they lack any of the redeeming grandness of vision, promethean ambition, and nobility of purpose and humanistic warmth of the nineteenth-century utopians.

The Lessons of Minayev

Given that most of this book is based on plotting an alternative revolutionary history of the twentieth century rather than on offering what Marx disparagingly called "recipes for the cook-shops of the future", the discussion in this book would not violate Marx's injunction against such "recipes". That said, if Marx sought to surpass the utopian socialists, nor is the tradition developed by Marx devoid of its own futurists. The discussion in this book is more in keeping with that mode than with nineteenth-century utopianism. Marxist futurism was adopted by the great Soviet development economist Yevgeni Preobrazhensky.

Preobrazhensky's criticisms of the catastrophic convulsions of Soviet industrialization saw him perish in Stalin's purges. In his 1921 book *From New Economic Policy to Socialism: A Glance into the Future of Russia and Europe* Preobrazhensky outlined a superior path to Soviet industrialization from the one that would eventually be taken in the 1930s. He framed his criticisms as a series of retrospective lectures written by an imagined professor of Russian history "Minayev", who is giving a talk in the "Moscow Polytechnical Museum" projected fifty years into the future – that is, in 1970. Minayev's lectures on economic history 'are heard simultaneously by workers in other places' – although Preobrazhensky's 1920s vision of the MOOC is based on radio rather than Internet technology.

Recounting a future history that never happened, Minyaev tells his audience how the 'New, Soviet Europe opened a fresh page in economic development' outlining this path through his Radio-MOOC (or perhaps better rendered as 'MORC'). Despite using the fantastical devices of virtual history, even then Preobrazhensky was never as deluded as Stalin and his successors who imagined that the USSR would be able to "bury" the West in an economic competition, as per the notorious boast of Soviet leader Khrushchev in 1956. In Minayev's final lecture, he takes us up to that point at which:

> The industrial technique of Germany was united with Russian agriculture, and on the territory of Europe there began rapidly to develop and become consolidated a new economic organism, revealing enormous possibilities and a mighty breakthrough to the expansion of the productive forces ... Soviet Russia, which previously had outstripped Europe politically, now modestly took its place as an economically backward country behind the advanced industrial countries of the proletarian dictatorship.[4]

The Minayev vision of a 1970s Europe that would have relegated Soviet Russia to a modest eastern outpost of a "new economic organism" helped condemn Preobrazhensky to death in the midst of Stalin's more conceited and parochial – not to mention bloody – economic vision of the 1930s.

In this book by contrast, Minayev's path is flipped. Instead of working backwards from an imagined future vantage point, we will work forwards from a key branching point of twentieth-century revolutionary history – the effort to spread the revolution to Western Europe following the Bolshevik seizure of power in November 1917. However, we should also not be afraid to violate Marx's injunction against utopianism. This is both by way of illustrating and elaborating the much misunderstood Marxian vision of communism and by way of flexing our utopian imaginations before they waste away entirely. More fundamentally, as we shall see later in the book, neither Marx nor Engels saw communism in utopian terms – which is to say as a perfected, static society purged of challenges, opportunities, struggle or meaning. Indeed, it would probably make sense to say that properly speaking, communism is not really a society at all, in as much as society is a relic of the Bronze Age that has lumbered humanity for the last 10,000 years – and a relic that we are still not strong enough to cast off, as we continue building ziggurats, both real and metaphorical, to megalomaniacs of every stripe and while we still grovel before our own social creations. But that is to run ahead of the argument.

Suffice to say here that if the argument in the previous chapter is right, then descriptions of a vastly improved future would not, in point of fact, fall to Marxian criticisms of utopianism. Here too we have regressed behind even the utopian socialists. For what will be described in this book is the future of the past rather than a future of ours. If the "common ruin of the contending classes" means that there is no organized social or political force capable of restructuring our society for the better, then neither scientific nor utopian socialism is possible, or at least neither is coherent. What would it take to arrest the drift of this timeline, and loop it back in an upwards spiral of civilizational improvement? Perhaps creative speculation about past and future has a role to play in such a process. In the meantime, we can indulge some virtual socialism built out of counterfactual reasoning. As we shall see, counterfactualism is not merely the conceit of us decadent post-moderns but a critical tool for political action in the making of history. We can begin by considering the historic context in which our virtual historical narrative will begin.

Franz Ferdinand Must Die

As we saw in the previous chapter, the First World War is one of the favoured arenas for counterfactual reordering. It is testimony to the irrevocable and overwhelming impact of the Great War on modern history that so many have sought to scrub it out of the historical record, or wistfully recounted how the July Crisis that preceded the war might have been averted. The British middle classes' compulsion to repeatedly imagine themselves prostrated before the Nazi jackboot across countless books of fictionalized Nazi invasion reveals a complex and grubby psychology of masochism and secret longing. The appeal of scrubbing the First World War out of history is more straightforward.

The *Belle Époque* that preceded the First World War was the era of airships, experimental new velocipedes, scooters and mopeds, the excavation of underground mass transit systems in London and Paris, the building of the Eiffel Tower. It was the era of the discovery of radium and microbes, of magic lanterns, cinématographes and paper-scrolled pianolas. New omnibuses and street-cars transported workers from the growing suburbs across expanding industrial cities, in which electric and neon lighting was beginning to replace gas lighting. It was the era of absinthe, feathered hats and top hats, crinoline and trailing skirts, elegant walking-sticks and twirling parasols. Jules Verne, Edgar Allan Poe and H.G. Wells had begun to imagine a super-technological future in which giant submarines patrolled the depths of the sea and stately airships would be turned over to leisure and mass tourism.

Liberalism was triumphant, stripping back overweening states in favour of a global free market undergirded by the gold standard and dreadnoughts of the Royal Navy, while European great powers were too busy industrialising and trading to fight each other as they had been doing for so many centuries. Political tumult was distant, peripheral and in any case vindicated the status quo. Revolutions in Persia and Russia (1905), Portugal (1910) and China (1911) variously sought to establish republics, constitutions, to extend democracy and build modern nations. Only seven years old when this era came to an end, the English historian A.J.P. Taylor was nonetheless moved to write of it that:

Until August 1914 a sensible, law-abiding Englishman could pass through life and hardly notice the existence of the state, beyond the post office and the policeman. He could live where he liked and as he liked. He had no official number or identity card. He could travel abroad or leave his country for ever without a passport or any sort of official permission. The Englishman paid taxes on a modest scale: nearly £200 million in 1913—14, or rather less than 8 per cent of the national income. The state intervened to prevent the citizens from eating adulterated foods or contracting certain infectious diseases.[5]

Nostalgia for the *Belle Époque* commenced almost immediately, as the great economist J.M. Keynes recalled in 1919 how back in July 1914 an:

… inhabitant of London could order by telephone, sipping his morning tea in bed, the various products of the whole earth, in such quantity as he might see fit, and reasonably expect their early delivery upon his doorstep; he could at the same moment and by the same means adventure his wealth in the natural resources and new enterprises of any quarter of the world, and share, without exertion or even trouble, in their prospective fruits and advantages ... He could secure forthwith, if he wished it, cheap and comfortable means of transit to any country or climate without passport or other formality, could despatch his servant to the neighbouring office of a bank for such supply of the precious metals as might seem convenient, and could then proceed abroad to foreign quarters, without knowledge of their religion, language, or customs, bearing coined wealth upon his person, and would consider himself greatly aggrieved and much surprised at the least interference. But, most important of all, he regarded this state of affairs as normal, certain, and permanent, except in the direction of further improvement, and any deviation from it as aberrant, scandalous, and avoidable.[6]

Even the terrorists were more decent back then, restricting themselves (for the most part) to assassinating political leaders rather than seeking to murder civilians en masse: US, Italian and French presidents and prime ministers, Russian Tsars and counts would fall to the anarchists' bombs and bullets; it never occurred to terrorists to target mass transit systems to express political grievance.

Yet it is the barbarism of the First World War that gives this era its retrospective gloss and explains the desire to squirt the creamy schmaltz of the *Belle Époque* all over the twentieth century. A world without the First World War is a world with more monarchs, a world with formal empires and colonies rather than only client states. H.G. Wells' science fiction depicting Martians exterminating humans as far back as 1897 was inspired by what humans had done to each other, after Europeans murdered the entire indigenous population of Tasmania en masse during the halcyon days of European peace. It is a world in which a mouldy old imperial Europe would never have given way politically, economically and culturally to the brash and youthful New World. It would be a world with far fewer (and much worse paid) women in the labour force, and a world in which mass military conscription would have been routine, racial hierarchy and colour lines more cruel, comprehensive and rigid, women's sexual unfreedom and domestic drudgery unchanging. Anti-Semitism would not be restricted to the political extremes but would be deep, pervasive and utterly unremarkable. Electoral franchises would be brutally restricted not only by gender but also stratified by layers of property ownership. It would be a world of lower economic growth, low wages and cheap labour, in which inequality in the wealthiest industrial countries of Europe and the Americas would be on a par with Brazil today, with all the oppression, brutality, violence and viciously punitive police that would be needed to keep such arrangements intact. This would be a world in which countless political and social reforms would have happened more slowly – if at all – and revolutionary communism would never have erupted.

If the appeal of imagining a world without the First World War is a hallmark of conservative counterfactualism, the nostalgia for the *Belle Époque* is also deeply ironic. It is ironic because it was the greatest and most determined opponents of the grand bourgeois civilization of nineteenth-century Europe who most actively and vigorously opposed the First World War before it broke out, when it broke out, while it was being fought, as well as the grossly unjust terms on which it ended. US president Woodrow Wilson won an election on staying out of the European war, only to take the US into the war six months later in April 1917. Lenin's Bolsheviks were the only political party that delivered on their promise to withdraw from the war immediately, to categorically renounce the expansionist war-aims of the previous government, and to repudiate the war debts accumulated by the Tsar. To wish away the First World War in order to stop up the communist volcano which blew up as a result, is to wish away the people who actually fought to oppose the war at the time rather than merely in imagined retrospect.

Counterfactualism on the First World War usually ranges the gamut from the absurdly trivial – what if Archduke Franz Ferdinand's driver had taken a different turn, thereby avoiding the assassin? – to the more sophisticated, focused on untangling the skein of negotiations, strategies, mobilization schedules and diplomatic memos that followed the Archduke's death. What if certain promises and threats had not been made, or worded differently? Yet the July Crisis that followed the Archduke's death was a whole complex of interdependent decisions, cast by a whole generation of elite statesmen steeped in martial values, racial pride, cut-throat diplomacy, limitless imperial ambitions and national conceit. These are the men virtual historians retrospectively expect to have arrested Europe's descent into war – the same men who would so casually send millions of their fellow countrymen to die over four years.

What the retrospective retuning of all these delicate wires of elite communication and machination leaves out is the powerful anti-establishment forces who had sworn to oppose the war – not during the July Crisis of 1914, but back in 1912 at the Extraordinary Congress of the Second International that met in November in the Swiss city of Basel. At this congress, this international organization unanimously agreed:

> If a war threatens to break out, it is the duty of the working classes and their parliamentary representatives in the countries involved supported ... to exert every effort in order to prevent the outbreak of war by the means they consider most effective. ... In case war should break out anyway it is their duty to intervene in favour of its speedy termination and with all their powers to utilize the economic and political crisis created by the war to arouse the people and thereby to hasten the downfall of capitalist class rule.[7]

While these labour representatives were attentive to the Balkans as a possible flashpoint, neither were they as naïve as to imagine that this was the only possible scenario that would lead to a general imperial war. They understood that great power conflict was inevitable: "should the military collapse of Turkey lead to the downfall of the Ottoman rule in Asia Minor, it would be the task of the Socialists of England, France, and Germany to resist with all their power the policy of conquest in Asia Minor, which would inevitably lead in a straight line to war."[8] If it had not been the Archduke, it would have been something else. The ultimate result – a general war in Europe – would have been the same, even if the war had been started in different circumstances and at a different time. The issue was thus not whether rivalries could be limited – they could not – but whether the governments of the day could win popular support for their wars.

Back in 1914 Keynes may have regarded the *Belle Époque* as "normal, certain, and permanent, except in the direction of further improvement, and any deviation from it as aberrant, scandalous, and avoidable." Yet he was smart enough to recognize by 1919 "that the projects and politics of militarism and imperialism, of racial and cultural rivalries, of monopolies, restrictions, and exclusion" played the serpent to his lost Edwardian paradise.[9] It was a period that was also gestating with revolution, not merely regression. Lenin welcomed the liberal revolutions in Persia and China of the early twentieth century, seeing in them the globalization of political modernity, a necessary step towards global socialism. It was not only politics. Every domain from science through to art was in revolutionary ferment, from Einstein's theoretical breakthroughs and the new science of quantum physics to Freud's pioneering of psycho-analysis, through the literary innovations of Marcel Proust and James Joyce, to the rise of cubism and Dada. While Keynes nonchalantly sipped his morning tea in bed and played the stock market in 1914, Marx and Engels' followers hoped to stop the war from happening. Examination of the failure of the International to impose their counterfactualism on Europe two years after the Basel congress and the Bolshevik and German Revolutions, will sweep us up to our branching point in the early post-war world of 1919–24. This will form the launch-pad for the construction of our virtual socialism in the next chapter.

Steampunk Revolution: The Second International

Marx and his followers were rotten at prediction. Or so we are told. After all, where is their fabled communist utopia? Yet as we have seen, Marx never discussed communism in any detail and claimed that it was necessary, not inevitable. As to the rest, the reason that Marx's predictions have never materialized is simply that they all already happened – and the left failed to capitalize on them. That was the story of the twentieth century, with the collapse of liberal nineteenth-century capitalism into corporate oligarchy, depression, war and barbarism. Too embarrassed to admit their own redundancy and defeat after having failed to live up to Marx's predictions, Marx's epigones today continue to insist that we are on the brink of seeing all of Marx's predictions about to come true any day now. In fact, we are on the other side of Marx and Engels' successful predictions, and therefore in territory that they left uncharted.

Their predictions that capitalism would follow cycles of increasingly severe crisis are well known, and vindicated by the Great Depression. But consider also their predictions on war. In 1887 thirty years before the First World War, Engels' prediction of a future European war was so uncannily accurate not only on the broad trends but also the details that it is worth quoting at length:

> No war is any longer possible for Prussia-Germany except a world war and a world war indeed of an extent and violence hitherto undreamt of. Eight to ten millions of soldiers will massacre one another and in doing so devour the whole of

Europe until they have stripped it barer than any swarm of locusts has ever done. The devastations of the Thirty Years' War compressed into three or four years, and spread over the whole Continent; famine, pestilence, general demoralization both of the armies and of the mass of the people produced by acute distress; hopeless confusion of our artificial machinery in trade, industry and credit, ending in general bankruptcy; collapse of the old states and their traditional state wisdom to such an extent that crowns will roll by dozens on the pavement and there will be nobody to pick them up; absolute impossibility of foreseeing how it will all end and who will come out of the struggle as victor; only one result is absolutely certain: general exhaustion and the establishment of the conditions for the ultimate victory of the working class.[10]

Yet Marx and Engels' followers fully hoped to thwart the march to war. Schooled by leaders who had lived through the revolutions and wars of the early to mid-nineteenth century, the international labour movement of the early twentieth century understood how war abroad could be used to suppress social and political conflict at home through the invocation of "social peace". After the Great War broke out, the suppression of class conflict would be known as the *Union sacrée* in France and the *Burgfrieden* in Imperial Germany. The Basel manifesto discussed above was designed to avoid social peace, in order to avoid a new Thirty Years' War. As we shall see, it was the Bolsheviks' shattering of the social peace in Russia that brought the Great War to an end.

From our vantage point in history, it is difficult to imagine the significance of the Second International's opposition to war. It was founded in 1889 as an organization to institutionalize cooperation among European and American labour parties and movements, far earlier than most of today's international organizations. Equally difficult for us today is to imagine the efforts of early twentieth-century socialists to oppose war. While today's anti-war activists have had as little success as the Second International, they go further in not even aiming to stop war, rallying behind slogans that express ethical disgust rather than political opposition: "not in my name". This reflects a world in which we implicitly expect efforts at preventing war to be resolved by large and remote international bureaucracies on our behalf, leaving us free to stew in our own moral torpor. This despite the fact that these bureaucracies of peace are led by precisely those states with the largest and deadliest arsenals, the most powerful armies and the most prolific arms industries. In the early twentieth century, anti-militarism was overwhelmingly the effort not of states and bureaucratic elites but of civil society – and predominantly of socialists and their political parties. It was taken as a given that peace was not something that could be left to states, let alone to great powers. Today, the peace efforts of civil society have largely been colonized by rich and powerful states as effective camouflage for their own war efforts, with humanitarian aid and development charities dutifully flocking to help pick up the pieces after war has broken out.

As political parties, the strength of the Second International lay not in pleading for alms but in the millions of votes they could command in battering down highly restricted franchises and in chiselling away at the prerogatives of appointed, aristo-cratic second chambers and executive, monarchical privilege. Its democratic power lay in the loyalty of growing labour organiza-tions leading industrial disputes ranging from California to the Urals and beyond. Their constituents were future military conscripts rather than the victims of remote human rights abuses. International cooperation was thus a structuring principle of labour politics, not least because anti-socialist repression in Western states fostered generations of political exiles who had perforce become polyglot, well-travelled international citizens in fleeing prison and repression. Today, internationalism is understood as a working principle of elite order, embedded in countless international bureaucracies, agreements, pacts, regional blocs, technical commissions and alliances. It is seen as the ideology of a peripatetic business class and their harried managerial cadre; it is the cosmopolitanism "of the front of the aircraft" in the words of sociologist Craig Calhoun.

Back at the start of the twentieth century, while their states plotted war against each other, labour parties fostered international cooperation. The aim was not the Lilliputian one of tying down state power by weaving endless cobwebs of international agreements but rather – for Marxists and anarchists at least – to abolish state power as such. Nation-building and state-building were the work of the greatest of the liberal bourgeoisie of the nineteenth century. This involved breaking up decadent dynastic empires into independent nations through revolutionary wars of independence in Europe and the Americas. It involved consolidating national home markets through trade, industry and urbanization and the spread of national languages. Where monarchies could not be tamed with constitutions and elected chambers, it even involved establishing republics. By contrast, abolishing the state was the historic task of the proletariat, according to Marx. If the great promise of liberalism has been to emancipate civil society from the state, the liberal bourgeoisie has repeatedly shown itself – even at its most cosmopolitan – to be incapable of abolishing even the ailing and senescent nation-states of Europe, let alone the state as such. Witness the congenital failure to form a centralized fiscal and political union in the so-called European Union. What was worse, the liberal bourgeoisie frequently renounced its historic mission to realize liberal freedom in favour of making money under authoritarian regimes. Thus the French bourgeoisie sided with the scheming Emperor Napoleon III, the German middle classes with the sinister Iron Chancellor, Otto von Bismarck.

Many decades before, globalization became the mantra of the

financial press, international socialism saw itself as the harbinger of a globalized world that was more socially integrated, more economically interdependent, more peaceful and with shrunken centres of state power to boot. According to Ukrainian revolutionary Leon Trotsky, rapidly growing economic trade and interdependence was bursting apart the nation-state and laying the social infrastructure of a new kind of society. Such a view was entirely mainstream on the Marxist left, and its protagonists were not management consultants but working class tribunes and socialist revolutionaries, their concepts more dialectical and sophisticated than the tautological nonsense spouted on the matter in today's academy and business schools. Yet this promise of globalization was being undercut by the world's most powerful states, which were locked in bitter colonial rivalries, competing alliance formations and spiralling arms races. "The West" itself was divided, as the capitalist class increasingly resorted to force to defend markets and profits. It was understood on the left that the very forces that had brought the world to the great global era of the late nineteenth century were now threatening to take it backwards: the logic of capital accumulation and growth was leading to capital chasing new investment outlets with gunboats rather than merchant vessels, and the restructuring of competitive free markets into vast new monopolies seeking to parlay market power into expanded empires with their captive markets and monopolies on raw materials. At the same time, ruling classes sought to deflect growing pressure on narrow elitist political systems by fostering belligerent and expansionist mass nationalism.

In contrast to this, the international left offered a vision of international socialism that was not simply based on defending welfare bureaucracies, sheltering from trade behind tariff walls, cracking down on tax havens, or arguing over levels of public spending and borrowing – glorified exercises in accountancy dressed up as politics. It was a vision of social and political transformation that would resolve the deadlocks of the current society in order to build the next stage of human civilization for the wealthiest, most technologically sophisticated and socially and politically advanced states on the planet – and through them, the world at large. That the proletariat failed to abolish the state is obvious. What is perhaps worse is that this is no longer even registered as a failure and a defeat for the left. It is a defeat that in fact only becomes visible in light of a virtual history of the Russian Revolution, which was an attempt to actualize this international project in the face of world war and murderous nationalism. The failure of this early project of political globalization – what Trotsky envisaged as a "United Soviet Republic of All Peoples" – has left us languishing in the condition of uneven and patchy globalization, with our political and economic systems persistently opposed rather than reconciled and sublimated on a higher level.

Zombie Apocalypse: The Social-Democratic Counter-Revolution

We teach school children that the Treaty of Versailles brought the First World War to an end. We show them pictures of diplomats in top hats busily striding about the gardens of French palaces waving peace agreements. In fact, it was Marxists who brought the war to an end – the Bolsheviks and their allies in Russia, Red sailors in Kiel and industrial workers in Germany. The diplomats scrabbled to keep up, trying to take the initiative back from the workers. When the Russians withdrew from the war after the Bolshevik seizure of power, they also undercut the justification for the war with which the Kaiser had convinced German workers to support him – the need to defend German democracy against Russian tyranny. With the Tsar gone and a workers' government in Russia, why were the German workers still fighting? The German Revolution followed, leading to the abdication of the Kaiser on 9 November. Lest anyone underestimate the power of Germany's workers at the time, the war ended two days later. Armistice Day, or Remembrance or Veterans' Day on 11 November, is a morbid, misshapen monument to the German working class, mistook for a commemoration of the dead in Anglo-American imperial wars.

Without the Revolution in Russia and then Germany, the War would have continued into 1919, if not longer. At their congresses in Stuttgart (1907) and Basel (1912), socialists had jointly pledged to prevent war by any means and if failing to do so, to turn the war into a revolution. Lenin, so often portrayed as an unprincipled and opportunistic schemer concerned only with power, succeeded in fulfilling this second pledge. Lenin was the single political figure who was in fact most loyal to the self-proclaimed goals of pre-war socialism. The Great War was a catastrophe for European bourgeois civilization. As the British foreign secretary at the time, Sir Edward Grey, famously remarked on the eve of Britain's entry into the war, "The lamps are going out all over Europe, we shall not see them lit again in our lifetime." It was equally a catastrophe for international socialism, as each European member of the International – with the exception of the Russian Bolsheviks, Mensheviks and Serbian Social Democrats – supported their countries' respective war efforts, in flagrant contradiction of their earlier promises at Stuttgart and Basel. That the most powerful Social Democratic Party in the world, the German, voted in support of the Kaiser's borrowing costs to pay for the war on 4 August 1914, left the party "a stinking corpse" in the words of Rosa Luxembourg.

Yet as we know very well in 2017, corpses have plenty of life in them. The German Social Democrats became the ruling party when the German Revolution erupted in late 1918. Had they been right when they calculated in 1914 that they were too weak to overthrow the German state, they had the chance to vindicate that calculation in November 1918, when the German state collapsed, the Kaiser fled and German sailors raised the red flag over Kiel. Instead of seizing power on behalf of the workers, however, they compromised.[11]

The Bolsheviks were castigated by liberals and Marxists alike for throttling Russia's infant bourgeois democracy in the interests of preserving working class rule, even at the cost of single party dictatorship. The German Social Democrats rejected working class democracy and revolution in favour of limiting themselves to a bourgeois revolution. What is worse, they helped organize paramilitary formations to crush workers' uprisings as well as the political organizations of the revolutionary left. They also openly fostered the nationalist myth of the "stab in the back" – the defeat on the home front – that laid Germany low. It was Social Democrats who thus initially stocked the organizational and ideological arsenal of Nazism. Railing against Lenin's dictatorship, the German Social Democrats built a new liberal republic in Germany that would go down in history as a by-word for instability, rickety compromise, economic collapse and misman- agement – the political antechamber to the apocalypse: the Weimar Republic. Having loyally marched behind the Kaiser to Verdun and Ypres, the Social Democrats would end up being marched into Auschwitz. In having supported the war in 1914, the Social Democrats proved unwilling to risk the movement for the sake of their goals. In the end they lost both anyway, as their newspapers were disbanded, their followers repressed, their leaders murdered in Nazi camps.

The German ruling class had hoped that a short, sharp and victorious war against Tsarist aggression in 1914 would help snap the loyalty of German workers to international socialism. They succeeded beyond their wildest dreams, dealing a body blow not only to the German Social Democrats, but to international socialism in the West as a whole – a blow from which it would ultimately never recover. They also failed more catastrophically than their worst nightmares, in that Germany's bid for super- powerdom would end up being defeated not once, but twice.

Their victory over the German working class would come at the cost of historical ignominy, fascist terror, many, many millions of Germans dead, the monarchy humiliated and overthrown, the empire dissolved and truncated, the nation laid waste, dismembered and occupied by all its historic enemies, its sovereignty curtailed and its great capital divided. German civilization throughout Eastern Europe would be eliminated in revenge for the depredations of failed German imperialism. For good measure Hitler would liquidate the old German ruling class when the Gestapo rooted out the aristocratic *fronde* that had sought to assassinate the Leader after the failed July 1944 bomb plot. Few countries' modern history exemplifies the common ruin of the contending classes as much as Germany.

Against all this, Lenin contrasted the principle of revolutionary defeatism. This was the idea that the political interests of the working class had to be clearly cut away from those of their national states. The logical conclusion of this politics was that the working class would benefit from the military defeat of their own countries. As war forced society to identify with the state, Lenin reasoned that working class political independence had to be preserved by opposing wars between states. The consistency of Lenin's politics with pre-war international socialism left him isolated even among those socialists who opposed the war. Seeking to salvage the promises of the failed Second International, the 1915 Zimmerwald Congress in Switzerland settled for Trotsky's formula of "peace without victors and vanquished" – a notion that was sufficiently evasive and ambivalent that it would even be adopted by Woodrow Wilson several years later. Nonetheless Lenin's steadily growing support among the Zimmerwald Left led to the core of a new, briefly lived left internationalism. This takes us to the next stage of our story – that of Leninist counterfactualism.

Back before the USSR

Traditionally the great "what if?" of Soviet history – the moment at which contingency is seen to be at work in the historical sequence – is the battle between Lenin and Stalin during Lenin's final days during the early 1920s, or subsequently, in the battle for power between Stalin and Trotsky after Lenin's death. Even E.H. Carr, the great historian of the USSR and notoriously opposed to asking "what if?" questions of history, was willing to countenance this particular "what if?" with regards to Soviet history. Yet by this point, the early Soviet state was already trapped in impoverished economic isolation and the political ramifications stemming from the decisions of individual leaders had been drastically diminished. To see more clearly where different choices had greater ramifications for international history, we can turn to the history of the Russian Revolution itself. It is around this earlier moment that this book reimagines the Russian Revolution and how it might have globalized, and the history of the twentieth century thereby correspondingly altered. As we shall see, a much more important "what if?" was Lenin's arrival from exile at the Finland Station in 1917. Without this, there would have been no Bolshevik revolution.

Although we retrospectively associate the Russian Revolution with the Bolshevik storming of the Winter Palace, the Revolution had in fact already happened in February/March 1917. In winter and spring of 1916/1917, strikes, mutinies, hunger marches and popular revolt in Petrograd, Russia's capital city during the First World War, brought about the collapse of the monarchy of Tsar Nicholas II. A shaky liberal republic – an interim "Provisional Government" – took its place, alongside a slew of spontaneously-formed elected councils established by workers and soldiers in the course of the revolt – *Soviets*. These emerged to substitute for the crumpled structures of Tsarism. Thus it was the world war, not Marxist revolutionaries, that made revolution inevitable and that sealed the fate of Tsarism – quite independently of the will of any of the major actors, Marxists included. Russia's ruling elite had hoped the world war would infuse the regime with nationalist fervour and expand the Russian empire at the expense of its rivals. Many of Russia's radicals and reformers alike believed that a popular national war was needed against German aggression. The combination of brutish absolute monarchy, grinding poverty and general backwardness, breakneck industrialization, urbanization and modernization made it plain to all clear-eyed contemporaneous observers that Russia would inevitably go through a revolution. To that extent, the spontaneous revolt of the factory, the street and the barracks in 1917 was predetermined. Where historic and conscious political choice mattered was less with the February/March revolution than with its aftermath: who would lead Russia once the Tsar was overthrown?

Many of Russia's new democratic leaders held to a fixed schema of political evolution in which liberal republics followed monarchical despotism, necessitating Russia's disenfranchised working class ally with and abdicate before Russia's numerically small and politically timorous middle classes. Exhilarated by the overthrow of a three hundred-year-old bloody imperial dynasty, Russia's new leaders, including Lenin's Bolsheviks, supported continuing the war effort this time to defend the vast new Russian democracy against the German empire. Meanwhile reactionary military officers and aristocrats longed to re-impose authoritarian rule. Terrified of the Russian rural poor and urban masses, Russian liberals and radicals alike variously entertained hopes of German occupation to subdue urban revolt in Petrograd, or else a populist, nationalistic dictatorship under socialist leadership in order to restrain the febrile new democracy. Russia's largest democratic party, the Social Revolutionaries – vast, amorphous and divided – were rooted in an economically polarized countryside while many of their leaders remained committed to the war effort and a liberal republic.

As was often the case in his own faction and party at large, Lenin was isolated: had he not arrived at the Finland Station in Petrograd in April 1917, there would have been no Bolshevik Revolution, as most Bolshevik leaders had already committed to supporting Russian liberalism and with it, the world war. Here is our first counterfactual – and one that is built into an uncontroversial account of the sequence of actual events. It was Lenin's analysis that diagnosed the contradictions of the post-Tsarist regime – notably in identifying a new, de facto basis for popular self-rule in the Soviets, even though the political leaders and representatives of the working class and peasantry refused to actualize this fact. It was Bolshevik propaganda that brought this contradiction to mass awareness that in turn provided the political support, legitimacy and viability for the subsequent Bolshevik seizure of power. It was Lenin's intervention – through the medium of his "party of a new type" – and the rapidly growing support of the urban working class that made actualizing these political insights possible. Thus Lenin's working class supporters began to realize that ending the war required not only overthrowing monarchy but the Russian bourgeoisie itself, which was in turn dependent on its trading allies and bank credits which a Russian victory in the war was needed to repay.

It was not just that Lenin's political intervention helped channel the flood of popular revolt but also that the intervention was critically timed. The Bolsheviks even worked actively to suppress a spontaneous working class uprising over the summer of 1917 (the "July Days"), on the grounds that there was insufficient popular support both in the city and the countryside to justify the overthrow of the Provisional Government, making any such attempt too narrow to be anything but a putsch. They did this even while their activists and party members were being repressed by the Provisional Government. The other factor in Lenin's calculation of timing was international events – and specifically a wave of anti-socialist repression in Italy and naval insurrection in Germany. These events prompted Lenin to say, "We stand in the vestibule of the world-wide proletarian revolution."[12]

Lenin's determination to seize power grew out of the intransigence of the wider left and was a political judgement on the historic weakness of the hapless and divided Social Revolutionaries (SRs). Incapable of carrying the weight of bourgeois democracy, the SRs also refused to collapse the institutions of Russian liberalism into Soviet democracy of the urban centres, even as electoral and popular support for the Bolsheviks grew dramatically over the course of the summer. Lenin's determination also had to overcome the resistance of his own party leadership. Here is our second counter-factual: in Lenin's words, "The success of the Russian and world revolution depends upon a two or three days' struggle."[13] Trotsky, Lenin's deputy at the time and the key organizer of the Bolshevik seizure of power, assesses the counterfactual to which the temerity of the wider Bolshevik leadership was leading and would have led:

If the Bolsheviks had not seized the power in October and November [1917], in all probability they would have not seized it at all. Instead of firm leadership the masses would have found among the Bolsheviks that same disparity between word and deed which they were already sick of, and they would have ebbed away in the course of two or three months from this party which had deceived their hopes, just as they had recently ebbed away from the [others]. A part of the workers would have fallen into indifferentism, another part would have burned up in their force in convulsive movements in anarchistic flare-ups, in guerrilla skirmishes, in a Terror dictated by revenge and despair. The breathing-spell thus offered would have been used by the bourgeoisie to conclude a separate peace with the [Germans], and stamp out revolutionary organizations.[14]

Here then we have the most determined exponent of Karl Marx translating Marx's allegedly deterministic dogmas into a moment of radical contingency dependent on collective, willed political choice: the fate of the world hinging around the outcome of a few brief days in a metropolis lost in the vast eastern, rural periphery of industrialized Europe. Lenin's calculation was spectacularly vindicated: in less than three years, three more imperial dynasties and their empires would be shattered; workers' councils would spread throughout Europe from the Atlantic coast throughout central Europe down to the Mediterranean, with Soviet republics established in Central and Eastern Europe. The red flag would fly over the Clyde, while a host of new nations would emerge across Europe, some restoring their independence after centuries of imperial bondage, others emerging for the first time ever.

Socialism or Barbarism

Rosa Luxembourg articulated the choice confronting humanity as that between socialism or barbarism. We had barbarism – world wars, nuclear rivalries, states engulfed in wholescale mass murder and exterminatory violence, racial and ethnic slaughter and pogroms, hundreds of millions of people uprooted, expelled and brutalized. Worse, socialism *was* barbarism. She foresaw this too, 'Bourgeois class rule fights its last battle under a false flag, under the flag of revolution itself'. It was after all her erstwhile comrades in the Social Democratic Party that crushed the German workers, and murdered her and her comrade, Karl Liebknecht – the only member of the Reichstag to vote against the Kaiser's war loans on 2 December 1914. It was not the perversion of its noble ideals that laid socialism low, but the suppression of those ideals by its enemies. This suppression required barbarism. Given how high the hopes raised by revolution, and how dramatic the stakes of completing the course of human emancipation, how pressing the need to end domination and war, it was unsurprising that the counter-revolution had to be so savage and fierce in bringing down humanity's hopes. Hence the violence and oppressiveness of Stalin necessarily had to exceed the sins of the Tsars: how else to command people whose dreams had been dashed?

It could be countered that it was the defeat of socialism that was necessary, not the supplanting of capitalism. The failure of socialism is the ultimate verdict of history on socialism's appeal and potential, whatever people might have thought about their futures back in the past. If this is so, however, then we would have to read Luxembourg's observation of the counter-revolution the other way round, too. In other words, we would have to ask, why was it that bourgeois rule could only be perpetuated under the red flag? Why was it that capitalism had to be rescued by those claiming to stand for socialism? It is well known that liberal capitalism had to be rescued by Stalin's armies in the Second World War, and then further propped up by the political acquiescence of conservative communist parties, who loyally followed existing national leaders in post-war governments. More than this though, the historic role of Marxism became not socialist revolution but finishing what liberal capitalism had failed to do. As described by the Italian Marxist, Amadeo Bordiga, Marxism became the bourgeois revolution under a red flag.[15] Across the twentieth century, it was self-professed Marxists, not liberals, who ended up fulfilling the ruthless task of building unitary national states out of pre-modern peoples, expropriating landed elites, shattering feudalism with civil war and revolution, ousting traditional leaders and religious authorities. Just as the middle classes of the nineteenth century thrilled to the exploits of Kossuth, Mazzini and Garibaldi, so too their descendants of the 1960s would thrill to the exploits of Algerian freedom fighters in the *Front Libération National* as well as Che Guevara, Fidel Castro and Ho Chi Minh.

The end result of the great efforts of socialism has been to revive liberalism. A doctrine designed to emancipate the European civil societies of the eighteenth and nineteenth centuries was absurdly revived to defend civil society from foreign totalitarianism in the twentieth century. The depleted ranks of liberal and even conservative ideologues have been constantly replenished by streams of ex-Marxists who, whether chastened, defiant or merely camp, have all conspired to keep zombie liberalism shuffling along. Liberals of the earlier era at least had the satisfaction of overcoming their own countries' pasts as they led their societies into the future and into modernity. Today's liberals have no such consolation: they can face down foreign enemies on the other side of their laptops whether these enemies be Russians, "Islamo-fascists" or immigrants stubbornly clinging to their cultures – but they cannot hope to lead the internal renewal of their own societies. That the life of liberalism was prolonged past its death should be evident now, thirty years after its victory in the Cold War, as liberalism crumbles under the blows of populism in the West.

All of this is to say that, if socialism has indeed failed, then so too has liberalism. Socialism was supposed to sublimate liberalism, to jettison its redundant flaws and preserve its great achievements on a higher level. It is unsurprising therefore that the failure to achieve communism was a common defeat for liberalism too. Instead of being pulled forward and transformed into something new and better, liberalism too has fallen back, regressed and fragmented. The political basis of socialism – working class rule and political independence of its organizations and parties – would be snuffed out across Europe first by Social Democrats, then by Stalinists, and then by fascists, although it would take the efforts of many more enemies before the ultimate defeat of the working class as a political actor throughout the industrialized world. This process would stretch many more decades into the twentieth century before it was complete. Lenin was clear that this happened in Russia early on, as he saw the Revolution collapse under the weight of its own backwardness, sinking into the convulsive dialectic of Russian history: imperial nation-building led by ruthless modernizing bureaucrats. Lenin's recreation of the old bureaucratic monolith of the Tsars led him to observe, "I am, it seems, strongly guilty before the workers of Russia" – an extraordinary admission "the likes of which had hardly ever been uttered by any ruler" as Isaac Deutscher put it.[16] Ironically, had the Russian Revolution proceeded as per Lenin's hopes, it would matter a lot less to us. It was to be the spark from which would spring the flame, as the banner headline of the Bolsheviks' newspaper, *Iskra*, put it – a slogan that was in turn cribbed from the history of liberal revolt against Tsarism. For the Bolsheviks, the Russian Revolution would be consummated in being surpassed by others. The continued historic significance of the Russian Revolution is testimony to its ultimate failure. So how might have things looked if they had worked out differently?

Chapter Three

The Best Possible World: Global Socialism

The year is 1924 and the Great War has finally burnt itself out, leaving a jagged series of truces and stalemates across a divided Europe. A war that began as a local Balkan conflict ended with the failure of British and French imperialism to suppress revolution across central Europe and Russia. Exhausted by their failed efforts and with mutinies and strikes stirring at home, the British and French ruling classes are desperately retrenching. With their imperious peace terms in the Versailles peace treaty having been rejected by working class revolt in Germany, they have lashed themselves together in a ramshackle new organization called the "League of Nations". Wracked by continental-scale industrial conflict that dwarfs even that in Europe, Woodrow Wilson has raced back across the Atlantic hoping that a Red Scare campaign against immigrants and trade union organizers will help him win the 1920 presidential election. The League hopes that the German Democratic Republic (GDR) – the puppet-state that they have established in West Germany – will act as a buffer to protect France and Britain from the revolutionary contagion spreading from Red Europe. Whitehall mandarins hope that a lull in European revolution will give them the opportunity to finally root out the guerrillas of the Irish Citizens' Army, as the ICA continues to wage war against the British-sponsored regime in Ireland. The British press meanwhile is consumed with panic about Red U-boats shipping arms to rebellious Glaswegian dock workers, while frightened villagers mistake looming coastal storm clouds for Red Zeppelins landing commissars in Kent and East Anglia.

Over the border from the GDR on the other side of the Rhine, the red flag flies as far east as the Pacific coast. Here, Russian and

Mongolian revolutionaries are still fighting to expel Japanese imperial armies looking to conquer resource-rich Siberia for the Japanese emperor Yoshihito. The *Deutsche Sozialistische Räterepubliken* – "German Socialist Council Republics" – of Germany and Austria, and the Soviet republics of Hungary, Russia, Ukraine, Poland, Transcaucasia and Turkestan are in discussions to politically solidify into a new socialist federative union. The great industrial and cosmopolitan port city of Danzig on the North Sea coast is mooted as a possible western capital of a new European federation. With universal suffrage, factories being run by workers and land seized by peasants, the revolutionaries of Europe and Asia are quietly confident that the next phase of conflict will bring about their ultimate victory as per the lyrics of their global anthem, "so comrades come rally/and the last fight let us face/The Internationale unites the human race." How did we get here and what happens next?

The Great Imperialist War

A prolonged decade-long Great War hardly sounds a more attractive option – let alone a "best possible world" – than a world war ending in 1918 as it did in our historical world. Yet this is more a matter of location than timing. The guns may have fallen silent on the Western Front on Armistice Day in 1918, but the British viciously decided to continue the murderous naval blockade of Germany throughout the peace negotiations of 1919. Revolutionary civil war rapidly followed in Ireland, Germany and Hungary, followed by the Polish invasion of Russia, and the apocalyptic violence of the Russian Civil War. The Greco-Turkish War of 1920–23 will inaugurate a century of barbarous ethnic cleansing in the pursuit of building purified nations. This is only in Europe: French imperial armies would level Damascus in 1925 as they expanded the French empire into the Middle East as part of a carve-up of the defunct Ottoman Empire that had been predicted by the Basel congress of the Second International in

1912. In short, in many places across Europe and beyond, the "world war" simply rolled on into new, sometimes worse wars – with murderous wars in China, Spain and Latin America yet to come in the 1930s. Unsurprisingly some historians think this period from 1914 to 1945 is better called the Thirty Years' War – a single seamless period pulsing with inter-connected episodes of horrible violence.

The possible world described at the start of this chapter is in fact significantly less violent than the historical world, not least because successful revolution in Europe precludes the sustained development of fascism and therefore precludes the Second World War. In this world, the "first world war" remains forever only the Great War. More immediately, bridging and linking between the German, Russian and Hungarian revolutions gives Germany access to the granaries of Russia and Ukraine, more food tempering hunger in Germany and giving people greater strength to withstand the devastating influenza pandemic that will kill more people than the Great War itself, both in this imagined timeline and in the historical world. Easier access to the outside world, less violence and general disruption as well as socialist Germany's help in restoring Russia's shattered railway network, will significantly help to temper famine in Russia when drought hits the Volga and Ural River regions in 1921. Far fewer Russians will starve to death.

A successful German revolution changes the balance of many historical factors at work. Workers' rule in the core of industrial central Europe would rapidly leave rural and distant Russia as a secondary theatre, with the shift of focus to central Europe sparing Russia the worst depredations of its bloody civil war. This would in turn allow Russian military aid to be despatched to the fledgling Soviet republic in Hungary, thereby sparing Hungary the counter-revolutionary White Terror and fascist rule that it would endure in our timeline until the middle of the century, to be followed by Stalinist rule until the end of the Cold

War. With revolution in Germany, Hungary and Russia, it is hard to see Poland limiting itself merely to restored independence. The struggle for Polish independence against Tsar and Kaiser threw up an entire generation of brilliant left-wing radicals who would help sweep Poland along to socialist revolution. This would scrub the Russo-Polish War from the historical sequence as well as the viciously anti-Semitic "Colonels' regime" of the inter-war Polish Republic.

In the historical world, imperialist intervention in the Russian Revolution in support of counter-revolution would inaugurate a terrifying dialectic of violence. The Bolsheviks prided themselves on the almost bloodless seizure of power in Petrograd as a mark of their discipline, organization and popular support. While over a thousand people died in the February Revolution, only two died in Red October. This would change as the civil war escalated. The same Bolshevik discipline and organization that made for a virtually bloodless seizure of power in Petrograd would manifest itself in a grim and relentless determination to remain in power against terrible, overwhelming odds and with terrible costs, "in blood stepped in so far/that ... returning were as tedious as going o'er".

From having abolished the death penalty in November 1918 over Lenin's protests and without challenge to opposition politicians in the first six months after the revolution, the relentless tempo of assassination attempts, subversion by a faction of the disintegrating Social Revolutionary party and foreign intervention by British, Japanese and US forces would all spur the Bolsheviks to tighten their grip on power with terrifying ruthlessness against enemies no less terrifying, infinitely more sinister and most importantly of all, lacking the popular support among poor peasants and suppressed nations of the Russian empire that the Bolsheviks enjoyed. Take the Baron von Ungarn. A New Age mystic, the Baron would lead a Buddhist version of ISIS in an insurgency against Bolshevik rule in Mongolia. Initially supported by the Japanese, he led his troops under the banner of the swastika across Mongolia and eastern Siberia while openly proclaiming his desire to exterminate the Jewish race in its entirety – all this was years before Hitler became leader of the Nazi Party. Inspired by the hell-scrolls of Buddhist scripture, he sacrificed the carved-out hearts of his prisoners to Tibetan Buddhist gods. The Bolsheviks magnanimously executed him by firing squad after his capture in 1921. In the timeline described in this chapter, von Ungarn's miserable, failed crusade is the last time that the swastika will be raised as the banner of apocalyptic militarism and global race war.

Back to Europe: assuming that Rosa Luxembourg and Karl Liebknecht escape their Social Democratic assassins, they gain the time they need to properly prepare a successful insurrection against the Social Democrats. Always a workers' city, a radical city, Berlin goes Red. The ill-fated Weimar Republic, a byword for political fragility and turbulence both in this timeline and our own, is brought to a blessed end, supplanted not by fascist dictatorship but workers' rule. Weimar does not last as long as even Kerensky's short-lived Provisional Government. The most obvious response by Western powers to revolution in Germany would be to continue the war with a full-scale invasion of Germany. In our own historical world, the Anglo-French High Command had planned for the war to last deep into 1919, not having reckoned with revolution in Germany. With the mind-bending hypocrisy of Wilsonian liberalism, the war could have been continued for the sake of peace and decency against revolutionary fanaticism and intransigence once the revolutionary workers' government rejected the imposition of peace negotiations.

Yet Anglo-French imperialists would find it difficult to sustain the invasion. Even US president Woodrow Wilson's liberal casuistry would eventually come unstuck in justifying the Allied invasion of a newly republican Germany in terms of a war against monarchical absolutism. Not even Wilson could turn a war against German occupation into a war to occupy Germany, a war against an expansionist imperial Germany into a war against a self-declared worker's state seeking a peace without indemnities or annexations. Even with the turbulence of revolution and civil war in Germany, German national resistance would undoubtedly only stiffen the deeper imperial armies penetrated into Germany itself. Having lost Central and Eastern Europe to revolution, the British and French governments would have to resort to detaching a buffer state from Germany, an outcome not unlike the one the French government had hoped to achieve at Versailles in our own timeline (instead they had to settle for a demilitarized Rhineland alongside a protectorate over the coal-rich Saarland).

Thus Britain and France band together into a League of Nations. Given the German Revolution, it is a much tither and militarized body than the one in our historical world, built around retaining the joint command structures from the Great War, involving much more pooling of sovereignty and institutionalized cooperation – more akin to an early version of NATO than the League of the historical world. Such an outcome is not unlikely: ruling elites have historically shown themselves quick to ditch their pride in national sovereignty when popular sovereignty threatens to escape their grasp – the European Union being only one example of this trend. Even in the world described in this chapter, in which ruling elites confronted stronger revolutionary forces, they still find it difficult to renounce the racial hierarchy on which their rule is predicated. Just as in the historical world, the League powers vote down a clause for racial equality proposed by Japan as an amendment to the League covenant. In both timelines, their racism constitutes a fatal blow to the League's struggle to win the support of the colonial world.

With the Reds having overthrown three empires – Russian, Austro-Hungarian, German – and having extended universal suffrage across Europe alongside the liberation of subjugated nations, they have achieved political freedoms beyond the greatest hopes of any nineteenth-century liberal. Having granted peasants land and workers control over production from the Rhine to the Urals and beyond, the new communist power is impregnable. The idea of restoring to the aristocracy the great landed estates of the Pannonian Basin or of East Prussia is as inconceivable as workers taking orders from factory owners, or democratic majorities bowing before the diktat of bankers. All this forces the League to cling all the more tenaciously to whatever popular and democratic legitimacy it can, desperately scrambling for members from the counter-revolutionary states of Europe, while extending fantastic promises of home rule to their colonies as a way of staving off revolutionary independence movements. League membership is hastily extended to White Finland, the Social Republic ensconced in southern Italy, Primo de Rivera's proto-fascist dictatorship in Spain and the Rhenish puppet-state, the GDR. Lenin, needless to say, denounces the League as a "thieves' kitchen" both in this world and in ours.

1924: The Calm before the Storm

This takes us back to Europe and back to 1924, as the League seeks to fortify itself against internal revolution. In Britain the death of Scottish revolutionary John Maclean in late 1923 after his health was shattered in prison by force-feeding – prompts the largest public funeral march in Glaswegian history, both in our historical world and in this world. In this timeline, the over-reaction of nervous police forces and a British working class emboldened by Great War veterans recounting their fraternization with Red German conscripts leads to an escalating series of wild cat strikes, lock outs, demonstrations and riots. Winston Churchill, notorious for his deployment of troops against trades' unions in 1911, orders troops and tanks to treat Glasgow as an occupied city. Royal Navy ships menace the Clyde and

Merseyside, their cannons trained on Liverpool's and Glasgow's turbulent dockyards. In the historical world too, Churchill as Secretary of State for Air and War sent 10,000 troops to Glasgow in 1919 to quell industrial unrest. A mutiny that same year would lead the HMS Kilbride to fly the Red Flag, and 100,000 Glaswegians marched in the city, calling for a 40-hour working week. This unrest began during the war in 1916, with rent strikes and efforts by the Glasgow engineers to avoid dilution. In the timeline described here, by 1924 the industrialized port cities of Britain's West are further inflamed by continuing bloody guerrilla war in Ireland, whose republican rebels are sustained by U-boats slipping past the British blockade of Red Kiel, helping to prolong the Irish revolution with guns and ammunition.

German revolutionaries correctly identify the GDR in the Rhineland and the Italian Social Republic as the weakest links in the imperialist chain. Given the overthrow of the Kaiser and the fact that the GDR is based in the heavily socialist and industrialized west of Germany, the only hope for this phoney republic is to steal as much popular and democratic legitimacy as it can from the revolution. With its flag daubed in socialist red and festooned with industrial sigils, the GDR's constitutional lawyers insist on abstract "democracy" against the reality of the producers' democracies of Red Europe. Such claims are threadbare, given that they are backed up by French armies and *Freikorps* paramilitaries. The GDR elite – a congeries of right-wing Social Democrats and liberal and nationalist politicians – squabble and intrigue among themselves and against a *fronde* of White Hungarian and Russian officers, exiles and aristocrats, while exiled German princelings lead guerrilla raids across the Rhine. Exasperated by the GDR's fractious leadership, the great Rhenish industrialists wish West Germany could find a unifying, decisive and charismatic anti-communist leader. They look southwards with longing and admiration to Benito Mussolini, who rules the Italian Social Republic as the fascist *Il Duce* or "Leader" – one of the great contributions of fascism being to bring the labels of school-children's playground games back to modern politics. The Leader maintains a brutal but fragile reign from the Campania through Calabria down to Sicily, his temporary capital in Naples.

In the spring of 1925, a growing campaign of passive resistance against French seizure of Rhenish coal merges with a massive strike wave to cripple Rhenish industry and paralyse the GDR as a whole. It is now that the German Union of Socialist Council Republics decides it is time to reunify Germany with blood and iron once again, this time under working class leadership rather than that of Bismarck. Never having accepted the demilitarization terms of the Versailles treaty, the powerful Red Army makes short work of the GDR's demoralized forces with its fast-moving panzers encircling concentrations of hapless GDR troops and French bases. With Rhenish workers welcoming Red soldiers, the French regiments stationed in the Rhineland are quickly overwhelmed and their fanatical paramilitary allies routed. The ramshackle GDR government flees Bonn for Belgium and Paris, escaping with cartloads of worthless Deutschmarks. Signalling the internationalist mould of the new proletarian state and its close relations with other soviet republics, Trotsky's Armoured Train arrives at the border with Alsace, welcomed and feted everywhere it goes. The briefly-lived GDR will be remembered as a vicious, militaristic puppet state, run by ultra-nationalist warlords, profiteers and black market smugglers.

The Italian Social Republic fares little better. Having emerged from the collapse of the Italian Kingdom during the *Bienno Rosso* in 1919, the ex-Socialist Mussolini does what Kerensky only dreamed of, establishing himself as Generalissimo of a militarized republican dictatorship after the flight of King Victor Emmanuel III to Istanbul. Beginning in the great Turin metalworks and Fiat plants in 1919, a colossal wave of post-war factory occupations and strikes across Italy's industrial north quickly spreads among the peasants who live in the middle of northwest

Italy's industrial triangle. Following a Blackshirt attack on the offices of Italy's great socialist newspaper, *Avanti,* the Po Valley descends into civil war, with working class anarchist and communist militias fighting together in an uneasy alliance against right-wing Italian veterans, Catholic militias, Blackshirts and *squadristi.* In the historical world, lack of political leadership among the unions and socialists led to the strike wave and peasant unrest peaking, cresting and crashing by 1921. One year later Mussolini established the world's first fascist dictatorship.

In this timeline, the success of the revolution north of the Alps provides not only a revolutionary hinterland of political advice and military support, but also the boost in morale and initiative in the factory councils, emboldening enough of the working class to overwhelm and sweep aside prevarication and hesitancy. The *Arditi del Popolo* rout the Blackshirts. Italian bosses, liberals, monarchists and conservatives establish the Social Republic in the south after the flight of the King, but its foundations are weak. The poor and rural south was always resentful and suspicious of the bourgeois unification of Italy from the north, more akin to a colonial annexation than a national apotheosis. The landless labourers and poor peasants of the south are as miserable under the rule of roving *squadristi* with their cudgels and torture devices as they are enchanted by the stories of rural occupations and the chasing away of landlords that they hear about in the north.

Terrified by the collapse of the GDR, and with peasants seizing landed estates supported by flying columns of Red *Garibaldini,* the fascist statelet of southern Italy collapses as Red forces advance across the Voltarno River. Ruled by a rump of decadent aristocrats, reactionary officers, fascist rabble and gangster militias, the ISR is a shadowy parallel of Mussolini's Republic of Salò in our historical world, which was established as a rump fascist state in northern Italy following the Anglo-American invasion of the peninsula in 1942. In this timeline too, a fleeing Mussolini is captured and executed by red partisans, his corpse strung up on meat hooks in the town square so that the people can witness the exercise of their popular vengeance. Except the town square in this timeline is in Naples, not Milan. The partisans are also more attentive to the corpse in this timeline – it is covered in quicklime and buried in an unmarked grave. Mussolini's dishonourable end may be no different, but Italy is spared decades of fascist repression and economic misrule, the civil war of the 1940s, not to mention the hundreds of thousands of Libyans and Ethiopians who live in this timeline, being spared Mussolini's savage efforts to bring them civilization with bombs and poison gas over the 1920s and 1930s. Thus Italy and Germany, two nations forged by the bourgeoisie half a century earlier, are reunified and remade by a victorious proletariat. With Mussolini's timely death, global fascism is stillborn.

To the west, the ruling classes who vested their hopes in Mussolini's leadership are devastated by his death. Churchill eulogizes the dead Leader: "What a man! I have lost my heart", he said, praising "his gentle and simple bearing and his calm, detached poise in spite of so many burdens and dangers ... If I had been born an Italian, I ... should have been whole-heartedly with you from start to finish ... in your ... struggle against the bestial appetites and passions of Leninism".[1] Demented by a hatred of communism that was akin to sexual perversion in its passionate intensity, Churchill helped organize the British equivalent of the *Freikorps* – the Black and Tans. Originally deployed to crush Irish revolutionaries, in the timeline described here, Churchill already has plans in train to turn these Britischer *Freikorps* loose in Britain itself. Thus the war in Ireland seeps back into the imperial core of the British state. Emboldened with Dutch courage in this world as in ours, Churchill comes to fancy himself a warlord in the mould of Mussolini. He is not without challengers. The Butcher of the Somme, Field Marshal Douglas Haig, fancies himself a British Ludendorff, and he tries pressuring the dim Emperor-King George V to boost him into the position of a de facto military dictator, much as General Ludendorff was under Kaiser Wilhelm II. These divisions within the ruling class will help the course of the British Revolution.

The End of the Versailles System

The collapse of the GDR and Social Republic coincides with a putsch by the Bulgarian military. Following the 1920 electoral victory of the populist agrarian party of Aleksandar Stambolinski allied with the Bulgarian communists, the repeated failure of bourgeois parties to make electoral breakthroughs prompt them to turn to a nationalistic military. In the historical world, the June coup succeeds against disorganized rural resistance due to the passivity of the Communists, the only ones who had the necessary organization and discipline to withstand the mutinous army. A belated Communist-led insurrection in September would be crushed by the military and thousands killed. In this timeline, the well-organized Communists intercede in favour of the popular Stambolinski's beleaguered agrarians. Better organized and disciplined, and well-armed by sympathisers in the military, the coup is crushed by Communists. Reactionary generals die in the struggle or are arrested, the Bulgarian Tsar overthrown and a republic declared.

Arms and advice flow to Sofia from Red Europe, allowing the new republic to consolidate itself, renouncing the post-war treaty system and the League of Nations. The great Bulgarian revolutionary Christian Rakovsky joins the new republic from Russia. Rakovsky was the quintessential socialist revolutionary of this earlier, blocked timeline. A brilliant polymath, highly intelligent, cosmopolitan and polyglot, he exemplifies an entirely different era compared to our more straitened, monolingual and nationalistic historical world – a crime for which he would die in the 1940s for his opposition to Stalin. Having trained as a physician, it was his experience as a socialist journalist across several

European empires that ensured he was well versed in the internal politics of many new countries' socialist parties. In this world, his internationalist vision helps to solidify the emerging Balkan Federation.

With the Bulgarian Revolution joining the German, Hungarian, Austrian and Russian, the destruction of the Versailles treaty-system is complete. It would take much longer to shatter in the historical world, and at much greater human cost. One of the first Balkan states to achieve independence in the nineteenth century, Bulgarian socialists looked to a pan-Balkan federation as way of sublimating the ethnic and national rivalries that had consumed the region, stoked by imperial meddling, grasping monarchies, sinister secret societies, nationalistic militaries and bourgeoisies. Bulgaria becomes the hub of these federative efforts, their magnetic appeal helping to disintegrate the neighbouring kingdom of the South Slavs. Known as the "Versailles state" this ramshackle forerunner of the ill-fated Yugoslavia will elude the grasp of an expansionist Serbian monarchy, which will in turn fall to the Serbian Social Democrats. Although Bulgaria will suffer a civil war in the face of opposition from the fearsome nationalist terrorists of the Internal Macedonian Revolutionary Organization, a process of regional federation and fusion will undercut the appeal of irredentism and separatism, as dispersed ethnic and religious groups can claim rights within the same set of political institutions in a slowly growing federation in which borders are administrative divisions rather than sovereign dividing lines.

Lenin's Last Struggle

A European revolution would mean a more German revolution, and a German revolution a more German Europe. This in turn would correspond to less support for national self-determination, as the triumph of German Marxism inevitably provides a boost to Austro-Marxist policies of cultural autonomy within overarching political structures, shorn of national rights of secession. Ironically, this view was often led by communists of minority and smaller nations. Luxembourg, who criticized Lenin's insistence on self-determination, was Polish, while Lenin, the Great Russian, remained implacably supportive of self-determination struggles. In our timeline, Lenin's last political struggle in his dying days was against bureaucratization and Stalin's consolidation of a personal dictatorship – a struggle which included defending the right of secession for constituent republics of the USSR against Stalin's more monolithic and centralized vision. All this was embodied in his 'Last Testament', in which he called on his successors to remove Stalin from power.

In this timeline Lenin lives a few years longer into the 1920s, his health less battered by the strain of defending an isolated Russian Revolution. But in this timeline too, his last years are also consumed with a strenuous fight – not against Stalinism, but rather for the global rights of nations to self-determination. Attacking the giants of German Marxism from a remote socialist outpost in the East, he is initially castigated and then eventually patronized as the great but backward-facing *starik* – "Old Man" – of the Revolution, increasingly out of time and too liberal in his concern for protecting the political rights of small nations in the new era of grand revolutionary federations.

In this timeline too, the failure to heed Lenin's advice exacts a political cost, as revolutionary governments come to terms with insurgent young nations seeking political maturity and independence although these costs will not be as great as the one paid in our world for not following Lenin's prescriptions. In January 2016 Russian President Vladimir Putin criticized Lenin's nationalities policy for supposedly aggrandizing Ukraine at the expense of Russia, thereby justifying Russian intervention in Ukraine's civil war in 2014. Only a century later did Putin – this ex-KGB man who declared the fall of the USSR the "greatest geopolitical tragedy of the twentieth century" – finally realize the depth and perfidy of Bolshevik treason to the Motherland. This, despite the fact that the Bolsheviks had declared all along that they were revolutionary defeatists. They gloried in the prospect of Imperial Russia being defeated, contained, limited, reduced and westernized, even to the extent of legalizing homosexuality in 1917, decades ahead of many Western countries – a civic freedom once again under threat in Putin's Russia.

The Foundry of Humanity

Exiled in New York at the time of the February Revolution in Russia, Trotsky remarked that he realized at that point that the US was the foundry in which the fate of humanity would be forged. US links to Marxism go back much further, with Marx himself employed by one of the leading Republican Party newspapers, the *New-York Daily Tribune*. Marx also exchanged letters with Abraham Lincoln extending British workers' support to the Union in the fight with rebel slavers during the great American war of national unification. More importantly, class warfare in the US had long been bitterer and bloodier than anything seen in Europe since the Paris Commune of 1870. Even on the eve of the February and October Revolutions in Russia, the US saw high levels of class conflict. The Lawrence strike of 1912 ricocheted across the American Northeast, raising the profile of the International Workers of the World (IWW), or "Wobblies" as they were known. Militant strikes in the coal, steel, railroad and textile industries alongside continued support for Eugene Debs' Socialist Party laid the groundwork for the explosive response to events in Russia.

Fear of revolution produced the first Red Scare of the twentieth century with massive government raids against the IWW, the passage of the Espionage and Sedition Acts, and the imprisonment of left-wing figures, most famously Eugene Debs, who had protested US involvement in World War I. When Wilson doubles down on repression by supporting the Western invasion of Russia after the 1917, anti-war pressure increases in the US. Samuel Gompers, head of the conservative American Federation of Labor, remained steadfast in his support of the US state, while trying to placate his more radical wing. Attempting to translate class conflict into racial division, local and state Democratic officials hoped to copy the example of the East St. Louis riots of 1917 and fomented race riots in Charleston, South Carolina and Greensborough.

Gompers opportunistically seized on these events to decry strike-breaking by black workers but, in the process, critically misjudges the course of history. In the short-term the conservative trade unions and large swathes of their membership remained openly supportive or indifferent to the labour movement's endemic racism. But the class-conscious, racially egalitarian message of the Wobblies's industrial unionism and of the Socialist Party began to see an increase in their formal and informal support. Famous Socialists Victor Berger and Morris Hillquit were elected to Congress in 1918, and would be again in 1920, along with a number of lesser known Socialists in states like California, Oklahoma and Kansas. The Wobbly-cum-Communist William Foster managed to bring black and white meatpackers together in a city-wide union. Their strike for better wages and representation quickly spreads to the railroad, garment and steel industries in the area. Lawrence and Lowell, MA, sites of recent textile trouble, suddenly go back out, reconstituting the strike committees of 1912. The racist Irish police of Massachusetts together with private hired thugs are sent out to do what they had done so many times in the past, alongside Harvard hockey students who go up to Lowell and Cornell football players to Chicago. The students are to put a respectable face on strike-breaking, much like they would in the British General Strike of 1926.

However, by the time the college boys arrived, the strike in Chicago had spread beyond what even the police – let alone hockey students – could handle. The success of the October Revolution was seen as an assertion of worker demands for self-determination. Railroad workers in Denver, St. Louis and Los Angeles joined the Chicago strike. Despite Gompers' continued attempt to prevent the strike from transforming into a general strike, the central labour organizations of Chicago splits, with Foster leading the more radical Chicago Federation of Labor thereby laying the foundations for the creation of what will be a far-left, communist Labour Party.

In February of 1919, soon after the governors of Illinois, Colorado and California declare martial law and National Guardsmen are sent in to get the trains back on track, Seattle goes on strike. In three days a central strike committee was running the entire urban economy. The Seattle police, lacking support from National Guardsmen who had been redeployed to California, cede control to a strikers' militia. The Second Amendment finds its purpose, as the armed organs of the state give way to the armed forces of civil society, the armed proletariat making the state itself redundant. In homage to revolutionary traditions, they call themselves Red Minutemen, after the militias of the First Revolutionary War of 1775-1783.

Meanwhile, class tensions in the South continue to simmer. Miners in Kansas, West Virginia and Tennessee went on and off strike. Black agricultural workers hold a series of protests for civil liberties and higher wages, but are brutally repressed. Woodrow Wilson, exhausted and still distracted by the desperate pleas of the bourgeoisie of London and Paris, palms off domestic repression to the military, pulling back troops from Russia. As National Guard and Federal military deployments finally achieve some degree of coordination, thousands of civilians are deputized in police departments from Buffalo to Seattle to Los Angeles. The municipal armouries created in response to the strike waves of the late nineteenth century are now opened up for plunder by the deranged middle classes of American cities, who rampage across ethnic working class neighbourhoods to terrorize blacks, as well as ethnic Jews, Italians, Poles and Czechs. As the strikes retreat in the face of this counter-revolution, horrific race riots broke out from Chicago to Atlanta.

Despite all this, the election of 1920 passes remarkably peaceful, seeing a huge boost in membership for the Socialist Party. Debs, still in jail for having protested US involvement in the Great War, nonetheless manages to receive 3 million votes – nearly 10% of the electorate. Fifteen Socialists are elected to Congress, as well as winning unexpected mayoralties across a thick belt of smaller industrial towns, like Butte, Montana and Terre Haute, Indiana. In Seattle, journalist Anna Louise Strong, a hero of the previous year's general strike who had connected the Seattle cause to that of the workers in Petrograd, won a surprise victory over the two mainstream candidates, although she is prevented from taking her seat by legal collusion among the two mainstream parties. By 1921, inspired by revolutionary activities in Europe and Asia, American workers once again see an opportunity to seize power over the bosses.

W.E.B. Dubois, ever supportive of black self-organization and union activities, used his paper *The Crisis* and his influence to promote trans-racial organizing in St. Louis and the re-emergence of militancy among southern black farmers. Simultaneously, the upstart miner, Alexander Howatt, leads Kansas miners against new industrial courts, legally constituted with the sole purpose of rendering strikes and boycotts illegal. Miners in Tennessee, then Colorado, West Virginia, Georgia and Montana, follow Howat's lead. Five governors declare martial law and send out the National Guard once again, confronting a well-regulated proletarian militia in the form of spontaneously-organized "Freedom Legions". Pitched battles rage across the Appalachian and Rocky Mountain ranges, with skirmishes, massacres, bombings and executions. Going onto the picket line and into battle wearing red bandanas, the Rednecks' fondness for dynamite will be put to good use in paralysing the movements of National Guardsmen and Pinkertons, whose columns are cut off and eliminated as they get lost in the mountains. The Rednecks recall George Washington at Valley Forge in resolutely facing down repeat attacks by sheriff's deputies, mine guards, state police and store clerks. The Battle of Blair Mountain in West Virginia will be particularly fierce, seeing the first use of military planes in the domestic US against organized labour. Both in our timeline and in the one described here, hundreds of miners will be killed in this most violent episode of US labour history as the mine bosses sought to prevent the miners from organizing a union.

Locked up in the mountains, these early battles of the Second American Civil War remain inconclusive until six months later, when steelworkers from Chicago to Pittsburgh walk out, followed in rapid succession by railroad, streetcar and textile workers and the now racially integrated meatpackers in Chicago. Although some Socialists stand by Gompers' call for law and order while tacitly fomenting racial divisions, this backfires, giving more support to the Socialists and the William Foster-led faction of the Communist Party. Their message spreads south to St. Louis and Atlanta, where W.E.B. Dubois and other black militants spend 1921 and 1922 connecting the black demand for civil liberties and equal opportunities with the same demands emanating from industrial unionists.

Although the Rednecks now rule across the Appalachians and Rockies, the railroad and steel unions each call a truce after having won major concessions from the bosses, thus temporarily leaving southern black workers in the lurch. Some anarchistically-minded Rocky Rednecks start murmuring about seceding from this United States of capitalists, to form their own independent workers' republics in the mountains, splitting from the decadent East Coast of bankers and bosses. But these mirages of detached workingmen's republics are swept away by larger events. Emboldened by the ebbing strike wave, the need rapidly to re-establish hierarchy and class rule leads to swift and violent reprisals across the country. In St. Louis 30 blocks of black homes and businesses are burned to the ground in an orgy of racial looting and violence. In towns across the South and West, nearly a hundred blacks are lynched in a span of two weeks, while reports of other massacres in outlying areas swirl as events move faster than the ability to report them. It turns out to be racial violence in New Orleans in late 1923 that unexpectedly triggers the next upsurge.

W.E.B. Dubois, jailed in late 1922 for having invited a group of German and Russian communists to come as part of a national convention on the Negro Question, had just been released and was due to give a speech in nearby Baton Rouge and then New Orleans. White rioters pulled a black streetcar operator and his mostly black passengers off a car and strung them up across the town, much the way slave-owners in the past had killed and displayed slave rebels as a warning. Black union members in San Francisco, St. Louis, New York and Chicago, outraged at the violence, called a strike in protest and, in an unexpected act of racial solidarity, find support among their fellow union members. Meatpackers soon joined and railroad workers followed suit. Demonstrating the entrepreneurial flair and individual initiative for which US workers are justly famous, the American working class begins to spontaneously form city labour councils to take over and run major cities such as St. Louis, Buffalo, New York, Los Angeles and Atlanta. Political authority begins to fission into two opposed sides – state power and that of the workers. Other workers see an opportunity to strike back at the bosses' hirelings brought out as scabs, with the result that more than two million workers go out on strike. This will inaugurate the final act of the US Revolution.

The tide begins to flow in 1924. The Socialist Party wins fifty seats in Congress, as well as the California governorship. Eugene

Debs, given clemency in 1923 as a sop to striking workers, triples his popular vote to 15 million. It will be Debs' last run for president, and indeed the last presidential election in US history under the 1787 regime. The next time Debs emerges as a national political leader will be at a constitutional convention, called to inaugurate a second republic. This new, socialist union will grow in time to absorb all of the Americas. The Monroe Doctrine and Manifest Destiny will thus be historically redeemed, finding new meanings beyond the intentions and dreams of their authors.

William Foster, abandoning plans of forming a Labour Party, instead splits the American Federation of Labor, taking large numbers into his new communist-led industrial union movement known as the People's Labor Federation. In the face of this challenge the Democratic and Republican parties finally formalize their elite alliance into explicit collusion, forming a Congressional condominium. Over the objections of many, though not all, Socialist congressmen, the Condominium pass a labour bill that recognizes the right to unionize and strike under certain conditions as they attempt to build a New Deal-style corporatist state in double-quick time under the pressure of events. They institutionalize wartime arbitration proceedings for labour disputes, creating a national labour administrator. It is the velvet glove over an iron fist: the Condominium also extends the Sedition and Espionage Acts of 1917 and 1918 to now apply to any advocacy of communism. Vast new appropriations are passed to fund the expansion of the National Guard and municipal police, and the army draws up plans to retake the Rockies and root out Rednecks in the Appalachians. Southern Democrat Senators block the US military from marching south, loudly declaiming how they will defend states' rights, while tacitly assuring Northern elites that the rural south will be left to the Ku Klux Klan to crush black revolt and union militancy.

Cross-racial union organizing will fight back against white supremacist militia in the South, but this will still need the support of Northerners, in the form of specially organized Sherman brigades that march south to support southern Rednecks, root out lingering forces of counter-revolution and defend blacks from KKK terror. Named for the renowned Union general of the Great War of National Unification, these flying columns are given orders to remind Southern Democrats of how General William T. Sherman dealt with the Confederacy. Despite the low-level bushwhacking war that will roil in the south, the major sites of the new American civil war will be in its industrial and coastal regions, with plenty of urban fighting as workers take control of the cities. Eventually the Mellons, Morgans, Fords and Rockefellers find that there are simply not enough people who will fight hard enough for them. America will go socialist.

Go West: The Russo-German Revolution Spreads to France and Britain

Back in Europe, the collapse of the GDR in 1925 provokes a political crisis in France. With the French economy propped up by plundering coal from the Ruhr, the Paris bourse crashes with the fall of the GDR. A tottering French coalition government hysterically threatens to rain poison gas and bombs down on the Red Boche and to annex Wallonia, as the rickety Belgian kingdom disintegrates in the orbit of the German Revolution. Once again the French bourgeoisie turns to an ailing Georges Clemenceau, begging him to return to power in their hour of need in order to support the faltering government of Raymond Poincarré. The sickly, blustering "Tiger Clemenceau" will come to symbolize the senescence of bourgeois rule in France. Knowing full well that socialism cannot be established by bayonets and that a nationalist backlash against a Red invasion will only strengthen the French bourgeoisie, the Red Army and Communist International make clear that they have no intention of rolling on from the GDR. They also make clear that Alsace will remain French.

Even a more militarized League cannot keep the Reds out

however. In this world communism-versus-capitalism is not a matter of geopolitics and diplomatic brinkmanship, but of internal social and political struggles. French socialism is over a century old, strongly rooted in the very same traditions that propelled the French bourgeoisie to power. As with all nations, class divisions are not wedges driven into a solid mass, but rather pre-existing divisions that nationalism is an attempt to suture. France will fall into a civil war that will closely replicate the geography of the revolutionary 1793 war in which the Church-riddled and royalist Vendée rose up against the revolution. In this world, a more urbanized France dominated by working class Communes will see the war tilt once again decisively to the cities, and with them, working class rule, although rural France will take longer to fall to socialism than industrialized England.

Over the Channel, the British electorate is more polarized since the splintering of the Liberal vote in the 1924 general election, not to mention a Tory Unionist government still fighting an unpopular war in Ireland to support the wilting Free State. Thus the 1926 general strike inevitably escalates. Called to defend the living standards of millions of coal miners from post-war austerity, the government's recruitment of middle class "volunteers" to strike-break sets up confrontations on picket lines that escalate, while anti-Irish jingoism roils working class life further. As the strike gathers force, soviets begin to pop up in industrial areas and quickly proliferate. A Communist Party already swelled by the prestige of continental revolutions and its opposition to the Irish war, grows in strength. In this timeline the British Communist Party will sustain itself as a major democratic force rooted in the working class, rather than what it would become in our timeline – a hang-out for aristocratic spies and louche Oxbridge radicals. In the historical world, British communism would eventually become an incubator for New Labour as well as spawning a generation of shady liberal columnists who continue to scribble away today for the *Times* and

Guardian – these last two perhaps among the most overlooked historic crimes of communism.

Efforts to use the military backfire as fraternization occurs between war-weary working class infantry and working class strikers and hunger marchers. Many workers already have experience of handling arms and infantry training if not outright military experience as a result of the Great War. This helps them to organize self-defence units to defend urban districts against marauding middle class militias. As the army goes red, the government increasingly relies on Black and Tans-style militias topped up with gaggles of six-toed blonde fops, ruddy-faced alcoholic dregs and second sons of the rump British squirearchy, who lust after the military glory that they missed on the Western Front. They make up for it now by terrorizing Irish Catholics and Jewish East Enders, massacring strikers and bombarding Britain's urban slums.

By the end of 1926, Britain is in full scale civil war across the Welsh valleys and the industrialized north and west as working class self-defence militias proliferate. The British revolution follows a familiar pattern as elsewhere: the crumbling of established authorities, the emergence of dual power, the security forces refusing to massacre their fellow countrymen as the government appears increasingly beleaguered and illegitimate. The "Welsh Wizard" Lloyd George, his notorious political opportunism only heightened by the severity of the crisis, seeks to save bourgeois Britain through extending the last minute compromise of a social democratic republic to the revolutionary leaders. But the hour is too late not only for the Hanoverian dynasty, but also for social democracy.

Churchill's attempts to redeploy the Black and Tans to Britain fails, helped along by Churchill's strategic stupidity and military incompetence as so profusely displayed some years earlier at Gallipoli. Heavily urbanized and industrialized Britain leaves capitalists with few supporters as the cities are dominated by workers. This makes the second English Civil War mercifully brief compared to the first. Remote rural areas and the Celtic periphery of the island are in any case firmly set against Churchill. The Welsh valleys remember Churchill's use of soldiers to shoot down strikers in 1911. This history, alongside the communists' expropriation of the great landed estates of Scotland, the restoration of common ownership over the Acts of Enclosure, the disestablishment of the Anglican Church alongside the abolition of the monarchy, the guarantee of religious freedom to the largely working class dissenting churches and promises of cultural renewal and political autonomy extended to the Celtic nations of the island, together are sufficient to win support even in the most outlying rural areas.

Within a year it is all over, as predicted by the Prime Minister of Great Britain and Northern Ireland, David Lloyd George in a speech delivered back in 1920:

> Four-fifths of this country is industrial and commercial; hardly one-fifth is agricultural. It is one of the things I have constantly in my mind when I think of the dangers of the future here. In France the population is agricultural, and you have a solid body of opinion which does not move very rapidly, and which is not very easily excited by revolutionary movements. That is not the case here. This country is more top-heavy than any country in the world, and if it begins to rock, the crash here, for that reason, will be greater than in any land ...[2]

The size of the working class population in Europe's most urbanized and industrialized country means that where the major cities go, so too goes the country. The tremendous concentration of capital at the core of a global empire – landed, financial and industrial – makes expropriation of the capitalists that much more easy and rapid. Britain's Hanoverian regime is ended, and after an interregnum of 266 years, England becomes a republic once again.

Revolution in the imperial homeland undercuts the need for the Third World revolutions to overthrow the Empire that we saw in our twentieth century. The great hero of Indian independence, Subhas Chandra Bose, tells Britain's revolutionary leaders that the:

> Empire stands today at the cross-roads of history. The Czarist empire collapsed in 1917, but out of its debris sprang the Union of Soviet Socialist Republics. There is still time for Great Britain to take a leaf out of Russian history. Will she do so? [...] can the British Empire transform itself into a federation of free nations with one bold sweep? It is for the British people to answer this question. One thing is certain. This transformation will be possible only if the British people become free in their own homes – only if Great Britain becomes a Socialist state.[3]

In the timeline described here, the revolutionary people of Britain heed Bose's advice, and the British Empire will be upgraded into a planetary federation of economically integrated free republics. The infrastructure of the global economy will thus not only be preserved but politically improved, imperial preferences and tariffs abolished. With racial hierarchies to be overturned, exploitative economic trading arrangements scrapped and political autonomy and cultural restoration guaranteed, many independence leaders across the scattered domains of the empire calculate that they will be economically better off remaining integrated into the global economy through their links to a socialist Britain, an industrial hub of the global economy second only to that of the US.

The failure to spur the British Revolution in our century

would dash Bose's hopes for a trans-continental Socialist commonwealth. Of India's independence leaders, only Bose was clear-sighted enough to take the failure of revolution in Britain to its logical conclusion. Instead of pleading for home rule through pitiful hunger strikes and campaigns of non-violence, he would fight the Empire directly. During the Second World War, Bose would form a fighting force for revolutionary independence in the form of the Indian National Army, composed from Indian POWs captured by the Japanese after the destruction of the British Empire in South East Asia. Bose realized that Indian independence could not be compromised for the sake of Britain's war with Japan. As the Japanese helped to arm the INA, he was happy to use their aid in fighting the Empire.

In the timeline described in this book, the sublimation of the Anglo-French empires into socialist commonwealths and federations will avoid the wars of independence that would be exacerbated by crude politics of partition. Integrated into the global economy through socialist commonwealth, India will see rapid economic growth much earlier, avoiding the low-growth autarky in which India was trapped for so long during Jawaharlal Nehru's rule in our timeline. India will also be spared Churchill's Famine in 1943, which will devastate Bengal much as Stalin had devastated Ukraine some years earlier. To be sure, the transformation of empire into socialist federation will not come without tumult. Australia for example, will see a brief civil war in the 1920s, as Irish sheep shearers in Queensland form armed camps around cities and launch commando raids against the soldiers brought out to protect scabs and enforce the bosses' rule. But the horrifying violence of partition would be avoided on the Indian subcontinent, and with it several Indo-Pakistani wars, as well as the terrible bloodshed of the Bangladeshi war of independence, all of which would come later in our century. As the empires are reconstituted as new types of polity rather than retreating into imperial metropoles, a whole series of appalling ethnic conflicts stemming from British and French imperial policies of decolonization are avoided in places such as Ceylon, Cyprus, Palestine, Yemen, Algeria, Lebanon and Syria. Without wars of national independence sharpened by Cold War geopolitics and nationalist rivalries, a whole series of inter-connected, bloody wars in South East Asia and eastern and southern Africa will also be avoided.

Back in time to the timeline described here. Following the establishment of the republic, a defeated Churchill flees with the some of the scattered royal family to Canada. Too cantankerous to hold together a monarchist government-in-exile, Churchill is increasingly isolated, much as he was in the historical world of the 1930s. Always haunted by depression, horrified by the elevation of Indians to the same status as white Britons in the new socialist commonwealth, he collapses into private life, whiling away his many remaining days producing mediocre paintings and drunkenly writing counterfactual history. In the historical world, Churchill wrote a counterfactual essay in which Confederate General Robert E. Lee wins the Battle of Gettysburg leading to the establishment of a three-pillared global Anglosphere divided between the CSA, USA and the British Empire.[4]

In this timeline described here, Churchill has more time to indulge these warped fantasies of racial revenge, white supremacy and a thwarted thousand year Anglo-Saxon Reich. He lives long enough to see royalist rump Canada absorbed into a larger North American federation. He is aggrieved by not even being granted the honour of being placed under house arrest by the authorities. He will never know that the success of communism has spared him the many further humiliations that he endured in our timeline, such as overseeing the greatest military defeat in British history when Singapore fell to the Japanese in 1941. In our world he would also have to endure the ignominy of bankrupting the British Empire to pay for American weapons and loans, and having to watch Stalin's soldiers claim the honour of actually beating Hitler. Thus in both timelines, Churchill's record is one of strategic calamity, military incompetence and ultimate political failure as his precious British Empire dissolves away.

Socialism, or Economic Politics

With most of Europe having turned communist by the late 1920s, what does Europe's future on this timeline look like? Would it be a grim period of authoritarian party-states honey-combed with informers and secret police, burdened by crushing political uniformity and oppression, public life dominated by sinister and romantic leadership cults? Of command economies, choked up with bureaucracy and dedicated to smokestack industrialization, throttling the production of consumer goods, with living standards held down in favour of producing tanks and rockets? Of borders policed like prison walls with guard dogs, watch towers and razor wire? And what would the rest of the world look like, when the imperial metropoles turned communist in the interwar period?

Even in the realms of the counterfactual it would be absurd and anachronistic to imagine that a communist Western Europe in the 1920s would be like a Stalinist Eastern Europe in the 1950s. Apart from the absence of occupying Russian forces, the sheer industrial economic weight of Western Europe would overwhelm the influence of pre-industrial Russia. Whatever it might look like, it would be Western not Eastern. This is not a matter of cheery dispositions, human warmth and sunny optimism triumphing over malice. For even the most obstinate official, grasping manager and imperious bureaucrat would not be able to solidify into a Stalinist hierarchy even in the Western world of the 1920s, even though it was much poorer in absolute terms than our own. Higher comparative levels of economic development, literacy, entrenched political and civic freedoms and a sophisticated and articulated infrastructure of democratic working class leaders and organizers is too thickly rooted to be displaced by any new managerial cadre of the post-revolutionary era. Authoritarianism, single party rule and dictatorship remains the malady of uneven and under-development and economic backwardness, and one of the core propositions of Marxism remains that capitalism powers both economic and political progress.

The model of the new democracy is functional workplace units that help erode the distinctions between private and public, political and economic, on which capitalist rule and hierarchy was built, as industrial democracy takes over the workplace, and political and civic rights are expanded across society. The new economies initially reflect national origins: Europe's southern tier where syndicalism and anarchism were more widespread sees direct workers' management reflecting a smaller-scale and more fragmented industrial sector. In northern Europe the more centralized and organized labour movement confronts larger, centralized corporate firms, making for a mixed, state capitalist economy. The mixture is different however from the wartime and post-war mixed economies seen in our world. The commanding heights of the economy – major banks and transport enterprises for instance – are run by the new proletarian state.

To say these sectors are "nationalized" would not be quite accurate, however, given that these new states are not only less bureaucratic and less remote from popular will, they are also quite simply less "national" as they dissolve away into new federations integrated into a global economy that will never be riven apart by the Great Depression and Second World War. Stripped of the centralized power of armed coercion, shorn of bureaucracy, democratized and decentralized, the proletarian state is in no position to swallow the economy. This not least because ownership of the rest of the economy is directly trans-ferred to the workers. Workers' ownership is institutionalized not only through greater practices of workplace democracy and electoral competition over management positions, but also through redistribution and issuing of shares to worker-owners in major firms and national concerns. Management is disciplined and constrained through practices of industrial democracy, while massive wage differentials are compressed, not least by increases in workers' wages.

Peacetime economies will see a boom in mass consumption as workers earn more and spend more, with enhanced social services providing further disposable income for the great majority. Drawing on Marx's guidance, the overarching emphasis of the new states is less on redistribution than on relentlessly improving labour productivity as rapidly as possible. How best to achieve this, and how fast to do it, generates disputes that grip the new councils, and form the basis of socialist political competition. The post-revolutionary era is not without other disputes too, such as whether or not to move beyond the Gold Standard under socialism. Plenty of left populists, radical agrarians as well as Marxists who wish to inflate away the savings of the middle classes disparage their opponents as "Gold Bugs" and Trotskyists, trying to belittle their opponents by associating them with a revolutionary from a rural backwater in the poor east of socialist Europe.

While the new workers' states unsurprisingly ensure that their urban and industrial constituents benefit from the new order with improved standards of living, this early transitional phase of post-capitalism will most strikingly of all enact a brief golden age for the global peasantry. Yet rather than heralding a glorious new dawn of rural life, it will be one last historic blaze of the sun setting on an entire thousand years-long phase of human history. Back in the early twentieth century, even the industrial world – let alone the rest of humanity – was much more rural compared to today, when over half of the world's entire population are fortunate enough to live in cities. In the timeline described here, with the global shattering of feudal property relations and the chasing away of landlords around the world all achieved well before 1950, the result would be something like a peasant utopia as landed estates are broken up around the world, and the ancient dream of the peasant of living free of usurers, landowners and priests comes true. This era will fade as socialist governments shrink the agricultural sector through taxation and terms of trade to help industrialize, while extending mechanization, chemical fertiliser, industrially-produced pesticides, irrigation and rural electrification over the world's farmlands, thereby allowing the consolidation and centralization of land-holdings as industrial agricultural enterprises. The children of this last generation of free peasants will leave the land even as agricultural output booms. Urbanization will have a much more rapid tempo in this timeline, with the global demographic tilt to the cities coming a decade or so before the end of the twentieth century.

The prospect of capital flight, which has so terrorized the left throughout the twentieth century, is never a concern in the timeline described here. That the left is so easily spooked by the blackmail of banks and multinational corporations only reflects how much the political vision of the left has shrunk to the confines of the nation-state over the twentieth century. The most that any centre-left party has ever aspired to is Keynesianism in one country, which failed to rise to the level even of Keynes' vision of international coordination, let alone that of global socialism. Instead of taking power in single states to mount tokenistic redistribution efforts or alter taxation, the internationalized working class revolt described here throughout the industrialized world means that there is nowhere left for capital to fly to. Its only escape is to be transformed into a new type of socialized property.

In our timeline, Marxism is recalled as a response to underdevelopment and backwardness, to extreme injustice and global inequalities, rather than being an internal critique of the most economically and politically-advanced societies. This was the reasoning, for example, behind the Kennedy Administration's "Alianza para el Progresso" ("Alliance for Progress") in the 1960s in our timeline. It was hoped that through land reform, growth in per capita income, price stability, extension of literacy rates, democratic government and economic and social planning together would undercut the appeal of left-wing extremism in the poverty-stricken, rural and deeply unequal countries of Latin America. But Marxism was not designed for such countries: it was designed to uplift and in so doing transform and improve the most advanced societies, the wealthiest, most politically progressive and technologically sophisticated states, building not only on the civic and political freedoms of liberalism but also the economic achievements of capitalism.

The fact that Marxism became an authoritarian developmentalism for Third World states is one of the greatest and least likely counterfactuals of the early twentieth century. It is also the counterfactual through which we are still living, and which we shall try to tackle further below. Extending the software metaphor, we shall see that explanations based on the software having been switched (the wrong kind of Marxism), installed inappropriately (if only it could have been downloaded differently), corrupted by malware or a virus (there is an authentic Marxism to be recovered beneath the corrupted code), or hacked (evil individuals pervert the course of history) will simply not do. To return to our counterfactual world, before we consider in more detail what a post-capitalist socialism would look like, let us consider how the revolutionary proletariat helps to consummate the halcyon era of nineteenth-century globalization with global revolution that will break apart national limitations on human and economic development.

The Short March of the Chinese Revolution
As early as 1853 Marx and Engels thought that the future of

humanity could be decided by the fate of the Middle Kingdom.[5] Evincing a remarkable broadmindedness for two nineteenth-century Victorian gentlemen, Marx and Engels' views of China's future were not down to any preternatural prescience but rather reflected their grasp and appreciation of the deep and interconnected patterns of human development, the significance of the global market, and China's crucial place within both. China's centrality to human development – by virtue of its demographic weight, its record of sheer exuberant inventiveness from the founding of agriculture through to industrialization today as well as its historical continuity and geographic contiguity – all mean that China is central to the story of human improvement across any conceivable timeline. It begins here with the Chinese Revolution of 1926.

In both the historical world and the timeline described here, the reunification of China begins with the Great Northern Expedition of 1926, in which republican forces sought to recapture northern China, which had been fragmented and dominated by warlords since the revolution of 1912. Bourgeois nationalist and communist forces were combined. In the historical world the Chinese communists, tightly cleaving to an alliance with the nationalists under Stalin's guidance, are set up for a terrible betrayal when nationalist leader Chiang Kai Shek turns on his communist allies, worried about their willingness to threaten imperial powerbases of colonial powers in Shanghai and Nanjing. Using his contacts in the Shanghai underworld, Chiang would shatter the communist-led unions and student organizations, launching a purge of left-wing republicans from Canton through Ningbo to Nanjing in an orgy of blood-letting that would approach Stalin's purge of the 1930s for its blood-thirstiness. While the failures of Stalin's Comintern policy in the West are fairly well known – notably in dividing the German left allowing for Hitler to come to power in the 1930s – his errors of policy in the East are less well known, although they may be equally if not indeed more momentous for the course of human history.

Stalin's policies were not only personal failings of leadership – there was enough of that to go around on all sides – but also reflected policy built not around internationalist politics but Soviet national interest, representing a growing caste of nation-building Soviet bureaucrats. Interwar Soviet policy was the start of a long and ruinous slide of the Soviet state into the pattern of perennial geopolitical rivalry between countries. Chiang's extermination of Chinese communists and decimation of China's coastal urban working class would lead Chinese communism to pivot to the countryside and with this, collapse into the millennial pattern of peasant revolt. This rural revolt will eventually overwhelm Chiang's incompetent, corrupt and violent nationalist regime after many years of civil war. Locked in rural autarky and led by a nationalist peasant millenarianism by the late 1940s, the stage will thus be set in the historical world for perhaps the single greatest calamity of the twentieth century, at least in terms of the loss of human life – the Great Famine, the result of Mao's disastrous attempt to industrialize China with force of will substituting for capital and technology. With it will come the single greatest paradox of the twentieth century: Chinese peasant communism turned out to be the only viable political and social basis for twenty-first-century Chinese capitalism.

In our counterfactual world, a successful European revolution not only avoids the political depredations of isolation, but also undercuts the significance of European imperial power in the internal calculations of China's struggle for national liberation. As revolutionary governments in Europe renounce their imperial concessions in China, Chinese communists take increasing command of the national movement. The armed wings of trades' unions are quick to clear Shanghai of the criminal scum that form a powerbase for Chiang. The Great Northern expedition succeeds beyond anyone's hopes, routing not only the warlords but rapidly over-running and absorbing all the foreign concessions, including Macau and Hong Kong. In our world, these imperial protrusions were only returned to Chinese rule in 1975 and 1997, respectively. The Great Northern Expedition is the opening phase of the Chinese Revolution as workers seize power in the cities, and the rule of landlords and warlords in the vast rural hinterland comes to an end. A desperate last attempt to prevent the growth of communist power by a cabal of generals around Chiang is foiled. Arguably even more bloodily incompetent than Churchill, Chiang's rule thus comes to an end, fleeing to the remote south, to endure an embittered exile and lonely death. Taiwan will thus never breakaway from the mainland. The brilliant Chen Duxiu, the leader of Chinese working class, retains his leadership role and becomes one of the most renowned revolutionary leaders of his era, Mao remaining a non-entity in the shadows.

The loss of China is keenly felt by remaining bourgeois states, capitalist governments-in-exile and imperialists the world over, as indeed it was in the historical world in the 1950s. In the depressed eyes of struggling imperialists, China's emancipation from white supremacy and emergence as an independent nation confirms that the white European bourgeoisie has 'lost the mandate of heaven' as the Chinese might say. They realize that their entire system of rule over the poor and the racially inferior is disappearing into history. The European subjugation of perhaps the grandest and most ancient world civilizations was a pillar of global racial hierarchy. In our timeline here, white supremacy ends a full two decades earlier and with much less ruin and bloodshed. Not only is China spared Mao's rule, it is also spared the ravages of two decades of Japanese imperialism in which millions of Chinese civilians would perish as a result of Imperial Japan's "Three Alls Policy – Kill All, Burn All, Loot All".

China is rapidly integrated into a single contiguous Eurasian economic space benefitting from German industrial and technical know-how as much as Russia. China's delinking from the global economy in the 1940s as a result of depression and war is avoided, and thus the foundations of Mao's murderous autarky are never laid. More importantly, Chinese industrialization and economic take-off begins much earlier than the 1980s, with fewer interruptions, providing a tremendous boost to the arc of human improvement over the twentieth century. Industrial Japan will fall in as the East goes Red, and in the timeline described here, a socialist Japan will bring about what capitalism has failed to do for most of the twentieth century: the overthrow of the emperor, and the establishment of a republican, multiparty socialist democracy with political competition.

The early union of German industry with Russian natural resources and agriculture acts as the engine room of a booming, unifying European economy. The dramatic modernization and industrialization of the Russian economy will far outstrip the bloody thrashing of Stalin's military-oriented industrialization. Russian development will be earth-shaking. With its massive agricultural resources never mangled by collectivization, its demographics never mauled by Nazism, famine, or Soviet economic and moral decay later in the century, Russian growth will propel humanity farther and faster than even Minayev might have imagined.

By the end of the 1930s the twenty years crisis is ending, the revolutionary tide beginning to ebb, giving way not to reaction but instead to new producers' democracies firmly established in the world's economic core and embedded in the urban enclaves scattered elsewhere around the world, mostly on the coastlines of the developing world. While there are still flare-ups of conflict and attempted coups here and there, and reactionary nationalist terrorism and insurgency in disputed borderlands, the social infrastructure of the new regimes – namely socialized property relations – have been decisively and irreversibly transformed in the core of the global economy, inaugurating a period of socialist reconstruction.

The global economy will recover strongly as war and crisis ebbs. The upwards thrust of economic recovery will be lifted and sustained by virtuous dynamics of a more integrated global economy in which borders matter less as producers' democracies federate and socialist internationalism displaces nationalism as a legitimating and organizing force. The political success of socialism, and with it the dispersal of national and imperial rivalries, the still-birth of fascism means that global resources do not evaporate in arms races and wars. The late 1920s depression is unlikely to be avoided even in this timeline, given the deep underlying structures of the global economy still grinding away even with revolutionary changes of political leadership at the top. But it will not be exacerbated by the tariffs and trade wars of the capitalist 1930s in our timeline, with a global economy fragmented by empires and failed revolutions collapsing into autarky. Depressions and recessions will soon become a thing of the past. Political integration and socialist cooperation ensures that policies are coordinated on a global scale, while working class political power ensures that living standards are defended, free movement of labour across socialist federations facilitating an economic flexibility and degree of freedom unknown even in our world of today.

Virtuous circles of economic growth, social advance, political progress, cultural emancipation will begin to intersect and reinforce each other. Infrastructural projects and investment occur on a larger scale as nation-states no longer jealously guard their sovereignty; the revolution emancipates women from church, children and kitchen enabling them to swell the labour force and undamming waves of popular energy and enthusiasm. This includes the rapid elimination of private and domestic labour: subsidized kindergartens, the rapid expansion of schooling, the provision of collective services for laundry, clothing and food preparation allows for woman's emancipation to advance further and faster in this timeline without the spur of world war. The artefacts of fragmented and privatized domestic labour in our world – domestic washing machines, vacuum cleaners and microwaves – are never invented for mass-production, as they are not needed.

The tremendous fillip that results from the expanding role of women reverberates across every sphere, expanding the size of the labour force and economic growth. New family forms will begin to emerge later in the century. As the family is no longer the refuge from a hostile and brutal social world driven by individual calculation, even the functions of extended family are dissolved into wider society, alongside new forms of civic associational and private life. Everything from partnerships for procreative purposes to artistic, sporting and other forms of liaison that require social recognition or sanction, blossoms. Gender matters less, sexuality is not suspended in fragile "identities" counterposed to one another. Deeper into this future, the debates as to whether gender is natural or social are decided in favour of the latter, as the continuing advance of science and technology allows a new breed of people to overwhelm trivial constraints on individual choice as hormones and genes. Needless to say, there will be plenty of challenges. A world that sees sexual emancipation come earlier, a more rapid dissolution of religious social mores and transport links not disrupted by world war, would also likely see a more rapid global spread of HIV from central Africa. By the same token, a more culturally and socially liberal world led by socialist governments committed to high standards of public health will also mount responses to help control the spread of the disease faster and more effectively, with greater humanity and warmth than seen in our timeline.

Deeper into this timeline, the world will benefit from the rapid and consensual technical standardization for scientific, technical, engineering and economic cooperation that will be the production of mutual agreement rather than enforced through victory in world wars and imperial might: socialism overwhelms capitalist autarky. In this timeline, socialism – a word containing the word "society" within it – retains its original meaning: that of the small state, with numerous state functions decentralized, dispersed and devolved to society itself, while the distance between state and society is shrunk through institutionalizing widespread elections to all branches of government, enhancing constituents' powers of recall and decapitating senior levels of state bureaucracy. The dissolution of mighty imperial armies and fleets not only frees up resources for more productive investments, but also at a stroke shrinks the state.

Thus the liberal states of the nineteenth century are even further shrunk into socialist states of the twentieth century. In our timeline, the growing dependence of private power on state power in the West was long overshadowed by the bureaucratic monoliths of the Eastern bloc. In this timeline, the state increasingly becomes the nightwatch-man state, preventing recidivist capitalist thievery. Forty years of uninterrupted growth, educational advance and political integration means that by the 1970s, socialism itself begins to fade. With such tremendous collective wealth, the remnants of capitalism have been drowned in a cornucopia of red plenty, making the need for even socialist nightwatch-men states increasingly redundant. With this, it becomes clear that the world is entering a new developmental phase in which the state itself is dissolving, and with it its opposing pole, society. With communism humanity emerges from both state and society. Capitalism, the ultimately transgressive society, transgresses itself out of existence.

The new socialist order will feel that the world has paid a grim and heavy price for its emergence from the anarchy of the market system in the two decades of imperial war, revolution and counter-revolutionary violence. Yet this world will avoid the multiple depressions and trade wars of the 1930s, as well as fascism, world war and Stalin's famine and the Holocaust. A whole generation of scientists will begin the study of the atom, of rocketry, of quantum physics, of demography, of gravity, of fission not as refugees fleeing dictatorship and war but in peacetime, propelled forward by immense investments by technophilic socialist governments and huge outlays on public education. Generations will grow up never knowing about atom bombs, MIRVs, napalm, incendiary carpet bombing, gas chambers. All this would seem not only horrifying but also inconceivably excessive and baroque forms of barbarism.

Further down this timeline, without the Holocaust and with fascism stillborn, the appeal of Zionism naturally fades away, meaning that there is never any decisive impetus to the establishment of an Israeli state. The *Nakba* – the "catastrophe" of the mass ethnic cleansing of Palestinians in 1948 – never occurs, while the Middle East avoids the whole sequence of Arab-Israeli wars. As socialist governments blast away formal legal restrictions and informal prejudices against Jews across Europe, Europe not only remains more Jewish but a second *Haskalah* – Jewish Enlightenment – occurs as Jews enjoy the benefits of political, social and cultural decompression that comes with greater access to resources, education and public life. Yiddish remains a major European language.

The Middle East further benefits from the success of revolution in Europe by avoiding the post-war imperial carve up embodied in the Sykes-Picot agreement. The urban centres of the Levant and Mesopotamia maintain their connections with the hinterland, a United Arab Republic (UAR) linking the urban centres of the Mediterranean coast to those of the Hijaz and the Straits of Hormuz. This UAR would be closely allied to an Egypt led by the liberal nationalists of the Wafd Party who seize the opportunity of the British Revolution to liberate themselves from the Empire. A byword for ethnic and religious conflict today, in this timeline the Middle East will be not only more peaceful, democratic and prosperous, but also more ethnically and religiously diverse, the benefit of its energy riches distributed more widely across the region. It will never know Ba'athist dictatorship, militarism and decadent monarchism. In this timeline, the halcyon days of Beirut are prolonged far into the future, as it becomes the financial and cultural capital of the new Arab Republic, as well as a haven-in-exile for counter-revolutionaries, deposed monarchs, would-be fascists, alcoholic aristocrats, White military officers and ex-secret policemen fleeing proletarian justice.

The success of communism in the West and the consolidation of democratic Arab nationalism of the interwar period means that jihadism never emerges. Driven in our timeline by the failure of Arab nationalism and cultivated by US imperial power and Saudi oil wealth, in this timeline there is no Saudi Arabia, no ISIS, nor any "Afghan freedom fighters", as Ronald Reagan dubbed Al Qaeda. Persia, perhaps the most politically advanced state in the Middle East since the 1905 revolution, succumbs to neither shah nor ayatollah. Preserving an upward trajectory of political, economic and social progress, liberal Persia becomes known in the Muslim world for the virulent atheism that it seeks to spread beyond its borders with all the imperious self-confidence of the ancient Persian Empire. Non-Western regimes remain nationalist, more class-based and socially and economically segmented than the Western core of the global order, but are nonetheless pulled along to the future by a rapidly growing world economy, global peace and rapid scientific and technical progress. All this allows for constitutional bourgeois democracies to evolve peacefully into socialist states as they economically advance.

There should be no such thing as society
Communism was supposed to bring history to an end, with the story of human development ceasing once we arrived in a

perfected state – the end of history, an idea Marx borrowed from the nineteenth-century German philosopher G.W.F. Hegel. Conflict, striving, division would fade away to be replaced by settled contentment and ease, with little to worry about. By the same token there would be little to motivate action: comfortable stagnation would be the order of the day. Nobody gets to be much better than anyone else, but at least everyone gets along at roughly the same level. This is all inevitable – so goes this schoolchild's version of Marxism – because capitalism would inevitably collapse in economic crisis, necessitating a grand effort of redistribution. Marx committed the sin of being teleological – thinking that history had a direction and hidden purpose, trending towards an ultimate end-point in which we would all be nicer to each other.

This Cold War-era vintage fable about Marxian communism gets things entirely the wrong way around. Marx said not that history would cease with communism but rather that it would begin. Communism was not the end point of human development, but its beginning:

> The full development of human mastery over the forces of … so called nature as well as of humanity's own nature? The absolute working-out of his creative potentialities […] i.e., the development of all human powers as such the end in itself, not as measured according to any predetermined yardstick? … the absolute movement of becoming …[6]

This view logically commits Marx to the notion that we currently live in the pre-history of humanity, or perhaps something like a vast purgatory of indefinite duration – a conclusion that he was happy to endorse. History, in the sense of the conscious self-development of humanity, can only begin when, in the words of Fredrick Engels, "The extraneous objective forces that hitherto governed history pass under the control of man himself." If Marx has often been criticized for being a teleological thinker, it would perhaps be more accurate to say not that he was teleological but that he thought teleology sounded like a good idea. Why not make the terrible contortions of history subject to human purpose, if such a thing were possible? If Marx was guilty of anything, it was no worse than many others in thinking that capitalism was an extraordinary social system – so extraordinary in fact, that it makes possible the subjection of the historical process of social development to conscious purpose. The paradox of Marx's communist revolution is that it is designed to put an end to revolution as a necessary mode of social progress – whether that be industrial, technological, political, economic, cultural – with all the terrible wrenching disruption and suffering that these uneven bursts of renewal inevitably wreak across humanity. Marx the communist revolutionary is the ultimate critic of revolution, the one who wants to end them once and for all rather than to leave us at their mercy. Given that communism remains for us only a spectral retro-future, we remain stuck with the irony that it is the greatest, fiercest and most systematic critic of capitalism who draws out the historic logic and implications of capitalism more fully than its most ardent defenders.

To brush aside the possibility of socialist transformation as fantastical delusion would itself be deluded in as much as it would be to ignore the stupendous scale of the transformation that has already been wrought by capitalism on the course of human history. Often conceptualized as a move up the rungs of human development, Marx's schema of social evolution could just as well be seen as collapsing the historical stages of development, by restoring humanity. Society after all, is only another way of saying that humanity is divided against itself: society is the web spun to ensnare humanity by holding it together across the internal cleavages that result from struggle over the means of production. Communist revolution would in this sense also encompass its original meaning – overthrow and transformation as the completion of a cycle. Most of human history since we descended from the trees has seen humanity cooperate and associate amongst themselves without entering into social relations – in the sense of having articulated structures of social control, divided into groups with systematically opposed economic interests, ensnared in complex divisions of labour and politically-enforced hierarchy. As socialism would dissolve away the divisions engendered by differential access to and control over the means of production, humanity would re-emerge out of this transitional form of post-capitalist society, in infinitely greater numbers and on an immeasurably higher basis of knowledge, wealth and collective integration compared to our pre-social ancestors. Society would thus resolve itself into its most literal definition – the people we choose to associate with. Communism is not only the abolition of the state, but also the abolition of society itself. So how might people have lived in the transition to communism?

Chapter Four

Lives in the Best Possible World

We do counterfactuals ourselves all the time – what if I had not taken that job, or met such and such person, or eaten that food, or not got out of bed today? At times the significance of a particular outcome – say meeting the love of one's life – seems out of all proportion to the contingent circumstances in which life happens. By the same token, who hasn't wondered about being in the position of those people who accidentally miss a flight, only for that flight later to crash, killing all on board? If we put counterfactuals to more serious use than merely startled or stupefied speculation, then we can use it to evaluate our choices when more practical and concrete exploration and testing is unavoidable:

> Why would we imagine alternative lives? ... If you want to assess your choice of partner, school, job, or car – or even the book you are reading – you have two ways of going about it. One is to try an alternative. This is relatively easy to do with books, as you can put one down and pick up another. It can work with jobs if the economy is good ... Unless your partner or spouse is unusually understanding, trying another one out for several months of comparison is more difficult ... Your only recourse may be to imagine what it would be like to have a different partner, school, job, home, city, or country. People do this every day.[1]

It counterfactualism exists as a heuristic tool to evaluate our lives and choices in the absence of alternatives, it is also perhaps an index of the degree to which so many of our choices are cramped and restricted. Psychological research shows that we resort to counterfactuals in our own lives when we are unhappy with our circumstances and previous choices.[2] Historical counterfactualism can also be a way of evaluating historical actuality: a yardstick by which we may try to identify the balance of necessity as opposed to contingency. It allows us to engage a more radically wide-ranging counterfactualism. This counterfactualism perhaps risks provoking unhappiness rather than helping us to reconcile ourselves to the individual choices we make in the limited range available to us. Such is the *Weltschmerz* of retro-futurism: sorrow for the world less because it is so dire, but rather because time is out of joint and the world is not where it should be by now, while we are left to make our individual choices in the darkness of shadows cast by the ruins of failed ideals.

Thus it would be a mistake to treat the various paths of social evolution as if they were merely crossroads or junctions at which societies collectively confront choices about which path to take; societies are not coherent individual units writ large but unstable amalgams of conflicting interests, groups and forces. Possible trajectories of social evolution are not choices that are merely confronted externally, but are built into the very functioning and evolution of social order itself. To that extent, even if such potentialities are imaginary it would be wrong to say that they are unreal as that would be an unreal characterization of society itself. For example: at a very basic level, a society founded on the principle of private property logically posits a society founded on its opposite – social or collective property – as a solution to the conflicts, divisions and oppression clustered around private property. If historical counterfactualism and extrapolation allows us to identify and draw out the conflicting principles that structure the very fabric of society itself, then it has already served to justify its purpose.

Likewise it would be wrong, however, to think that counterfactual reasoning in history is a straightforward case of scaling up from the individual counterfactual assessments of one's own life to the social level. Of the many issues involved in making this shift is that it concerns a scale of change over events and factors that we rarely if ever directly control – the matrix within which we make individual decisions. Taking Lebow's consumer-oriented examples, these would be not only merely choosing between cars but whether or not we have flying cars to choose between – surely the basic standard of any future worth having. This is not to say that the historical process is indifferent to specific individual choices, such as the outlooks and backgrounds of political leaders. Yet it is safe to say frequently that had one particular leader not appeared, these social forces would have manifested themselves in others of the same ilk: there were plenty of fascists besides Hitler. For that reason, the greater the control that humanity has over its social institutions, the more scope and possibility for the individual to escape the domination of social forces, the more difficult it would become for us to make inferences about the kind of people that would inhabit such a world.

Thus it makes sense to restrict counterfactual biography to the lives of those previous generations that were historically closest to the changes that we are discussing. Doing it this way makes it easier to imagine how their lives might have unfolded differently in improved circumstances. At the same time, this allows us to better understand the forces shaping these people's lives. The lives of my own family of that time illustrate how individual lives are affected by these larger historical developments.

Prosopography: Personal and Revolutionary
Even my family's ordinary lives – far from any centres of decision-making – dramatically illustrate the misery and hardship resulting from capitalist collapse, civil war, stalled and abortive revolutions across Europe. With my paternal grand-

parents born to working class families in the midst of the First World War, they came of age in an era in which adulthood began earlier – in the depression and on the brink of renewed global warfare. Fleeing a broken home and unable to find work in the midst of the depression, my grandfather roamed the countryside picking up odd jobs on farms and construction sites, avoiding the alcoholism that consumed many of the itinerant and hungry unemployed of depression-era England. It was only when he joined a local regiment in the midst of Britain's rearmament drive in the 1930s that hunger and unemployment was abolished for him. Despite this bleak early life, in other ways he was lucky. He was taken in by kindly neighbours as an adolescent after his family home disintegrated. His two closest army comrades both lost limbs in the retreat to Dunkirk, while he only lost his hearing. He thus earned an honourable discharge and avoided deployment with his regiment to Tunisia and Italy (although the army refused him a disability pension, refusing to recognize his battle-induced deafness as a war-inflicted disability). Health problems would grant him early retirement from his subsequent work as a coker in a steel foundry, thereby likely sparing him death from the cancer to which many of his workmates succumbed, and which he attributed to the long shifts in filthy working conditions of toxic dust and fumes in British Steel.

Revolution in Europe that helped consolidate workers' rule across Europe would have meliorated if not entirely nullified the ravages of the depression by protecting working class living standards. The world war and the crushing austerity that followed it – in which the government screwed down working class consumption in order to pay off war-time debts and hold onto the empire – would have been avoided. Our better world would have likely meant better health, less physical and economic hardship for my grandfather, as well as more leisure and a significantly higher standard of living significantly earlier. Perhaps it could have meant a wider horizon too. Despite having left school at 14, he voraciously consumed studies of history that would put his better-educated grandson to shame. Perhaps a working class government investing in further education may have created outlets for his intellectual interests. It is difficult to see how he might have met my grandmother in this world, given that they were introduced through a mutual friend he met while unemployed, and given that my grandmother was also sucked into – and indeed almost killed – in the poorly regulated wartime industries of northern England.

Although my maternal grandparents were born later, their lives were no less shaped by the violent ravages of that period on the other side of Europe. My grandmother's girlhood and early adolescence was spent under Nazi bombs and occupation in Serbia: she recalled a German officer billeted with her family offering her and her friend slices of orange, a relatively exotic fruit at that time that in all likelihood came from the notorious German plunder of the Greek orange harvest during the Nazi occupation of that country. She would lose her father in the chaos of occupation and civil war that followed. Kidnapped during winter by royalist Serbian guerrillas – *četniks* – for reasons that are obscure, they threatened to cut his wife's throat when she pleaded with them to at least let her give him an overcoat to protect him from the cold. It was no idle threat: my great-grandmother had already had cousins – both men and women – massacred by *četniks* in a nearby village. Although her husband returned six weeks later, his health was shattered by exposure and he died shortly thereafter.

The victory of Tito's partisans in that war opened up opportunities. As mass education was a priority for modernizing, developmental states engaged in forming centralized nation-states out of fragmented ethnic groups, my grandmother trained as a primary and high school teacher – something that her stern father would have forbidden her in the old Yugoslav kingdom, opposed as he was to women's education. Her new job involved being posted to remote hamlets in the course of which she met my grandfather, who although having a working class rather than rural background, was also swept up in the post-war modernization and education drive. In the better world outlined in previous chapters, they would have both avoided the war and Yugoslav dictatorship, first under Serbian monarchy and then under Tito's single-party rule. If particularly vocationally suited and predisposed to teaching, they would doubtless have had opportunities to pursue this in a larger Balkan federation that would have likely invested heavily in raising living standards through mass education and rural integration. It is not inconceivable that my grandparents might still have met in such circumstances. Regardless, their lives would have also benefitted from higher economic growth in Europe and the region as a whole, with a higher standard of living earlier, quicker cultural change and political openness compared to the grim early decades of Tito's rule. They would also have been spared war at both ends of their lives. My grandfather resigned his membership of the Yugoslav communist party in disgust at the drift of politics towards the end of the 1980s, although he didn't live long enough to see the collapse of the united Yugoslavia for which he had fought when he joined Tito's partisans as a teenager.

In our better world, a larger Balkan federation less rooted in South Slav nationalism would have avoided Tito's convoluted and authoritarian nationalities policy, which took the logic of Stalin's socialism-in-one-country to its ultimate end-point. In the story of the Cold War, Tito is often cast as an uppity rebel against Soviet domination after he broke with Stalin in 1948. In fact, Tito was always *plus royaliste que le roi* when it came to following the Georgian dictator. After all, Tito's assertion of the "Yugoslav road to socialism" against Moscow was only following the logic of Stalin's "socialism in one country" to its conclusion. Tito's revolt would prompt the post-war fractalization of Stalinism, as each new revolutionary leader across the developing world began building his own national road to socialism. Unsurprisingly this story ended not with global socialism but only with more countries, more borders, more geopolitics, more absurdly concocted stories of national conceit and glory, more fragmentation of humanity.

With Titoism, the originary socialism in one country replicates in ever smaller and more absurd forms, each new state seeking to duplicate the Stalinist model of rapid national modernization, industrialization and military strength that would allow it to shake off imperial bondage and compete with its neighbours. Thus Stalinism gushed forth in sundry and ever-pettier varieties. Arab socialism became Egyptian, Syrian, Libyan and Yemeni socialism; European became Russian, Yugoslav, Hungarian, Romanian and Albanian socialism, African socialism became Ghanaian, Tanzanian and Burkinabe socialism, Asian became Chinese, Cambodian, Vietnamese, Burmese socialism. Given that most of these countries were rural backwaters dependent on export of food and raw materials in the global economy, it should hardly be a surprise that they usually ended up being led by authoritarian strongmen draped in brocade and wearing big boots, not unlike Tito himself. Yet this generation of leaders nonetheless succeeded where capitalist imperialism had failed, in ruthlessly ensuring that their newly-established countries were made properly ready for global capitalism. The "socialism with Chinese characteristics" of today is, after all, only high-tech Victorian-style industrialization with Chinese characteristics.

The end result of Tito's Stalinism can be seen by looking at the map of the so-called "Western Balkans" today: a clutch of small, mostly ethnically homogenous EU/NATO protectorates whose long and winding new borders defy economic rationality, linguistic sense, and political dignity and civility. My grandmother would live through the dislocation of the Yugoslav wars of secession across the 1990s, witnessing hyperinflation, deindustrialization and the rapid rise of deep poverty as pensions evaporated and medicines disappeared under a United Nations sanctions regime. She would also see the return of the Luftwaffe to Balkan skies with the NATO bombing campaign of 1999. In our better world, a larger Balkan federation would not only have avoided the horrors of fascism and civil war, but a socialist Europe which saw growing political convergence, enhanced openness and economic growth would have found the political confidence and social capacities to blend away rather than indulge jealous nationalisms.

Political Leaders

As the changes discussed in previous chapters have been politically-driven, it makes sense to consider the counterfactual biographies of major political figures. Some of these – Lenin, Trotsky, Luxembourg, Mussolini, Churchill, Chiang Kai-shek – we have dealt with already in the course of the counterfactual narrative. Others would have never had the chance to develop political careers or would have been propelled in different trajectories. Stalin was already a senior if publicly unknown Bolshevik by the time of the Russian Revolution, with little independent political authority. Without the isolation and internalization of the revolution, he would never had been put into a position to lead the bureaucratic ossification of the early Soviet state. An assiduous and capable administrator, well versed in the national rivalries and ethnic intrigues that roiled the periphery of the old Tsarist empire, in this world he would have been absorbed in the tasks of national development and modernization in Soviet Transcaucasia and Turkestan – a job that would doubtless have provided plenty of opportunity for him to indulge the exercise of personal power and bureaucratic intrigue which he found so satisfying. However much power he managed to accumulate, the might of a Western revolution would overwhelm the individual designs of any individual bureaucrat, however malevolent or powerful in a remote eastern outpost of a larger federation.

Although secretly jealous of more dashing and renowned figures such as Trotsky, Stalin must pay obeisance to Trotsky's success as military leader and revolutionary organizer, the grim Georgian remaining a loyal Trotskyist to his dying day in the late 1950s.

With the success of the revolution in Europe, an entire generation of revolutionary leaders survive, never falling to fascism or Stalinism. Tough, brilliant, multilingual, versed in institutional coordination and design from cumulative decades of work in political parties, journalism, industrial unionizing and shop-floor militancy, these figures are available in this world to help accelerate and propel revolution and post-revolutionary reconstruction. In this world, the success of the revolution in the West means paradoxically that a whole generation of revolutionary figures in the Third World are absent. Successful revolution in the West accelerates and consummates the globalizing processes of capitalism. Without the need to protect private property and the hierarchical social order associated with it, the nation-state shrinks in the West, and is never spread to the formerly colonial world. Africans benefit from being able to leap over the nation-state as a necessary political form of development. Africa turns out to be a country, after all.

A whole generation of founding fathers of independent nations never emerge – the names of Ho Chi Minh, Ahmed Ben Bella, Kwame Nkrumah, Eric Williams, Kim Il Sung, Sukarno will be unknown in this world. Post-colonial revolt will not be the only revolutionary after-shock whose purpose is thwarted by Marxist revolution in the core. So too, feminism and civil rights become redundant in this improved twentieth century. The course of revolution achieves in a few bloody years what would take decades of bloody struggle in our twentieth century, while the uplift of women through workplace militancy, unionization as well as the formal policies enacted by post-revolutionary governments achieves in a handful of years what would again, take decades in our twentieth century. Socialist governments everywhere deliver suffrage, access to contraception, abortion on demand, public child care, access to all levels of education, as well as the liberalization of divorce laws and the expansion of women's rights to dispose of and transfer personal property. Feminism and post-colonial movements, both responses to the stunting and failure of revolution in our world, never emerge in this better world.

Similarly another generation of romantic revolutionaries, national leaders and modernizers never emerges to challenge imperialism because imperialism, having been defeated in the core, never needs to be challenged in the periphery. Figures like Fidel Castro, Che Guevara, Gamel Abdul Nasser find other outlets for their undoubted talents and instinct for leadership as they are swept along with the waves of vertiginous social mobility, booming economic growth and rapid technological modernization that begins to wash across the world decades earlier in this timeline. Other would-be Third World leaders are freed to devote time to other pursuits. As India modernizes, the Green Revolution comes decades earlier, thereby diminishing the appeal of Gandhi's suggestion that Indians fast in order to reduce hunger. Sidelined in the newly independent India by more clear-sighted and modernizing leaders such as B.R. Ambedkar and Subhas Bose, Gandhi has more time to indulge his other pursuits such as receiving more enemas from his teenaged female followers. He also notoriously enjoys practising "sexual restraint" by cuddling naked with them in bed. Gandhi's philosophy appeals to some middle-class wasters who are repulsed by modern technology, but otherwise Gandhi's influence remains mercifully marginal in this world, which has overcome war not through mystical invocations of non-violence but through revolutionary political change and economic advance.

Other political figures may well have found their private lives to be more emancipated under socialism than their public lives were under capitalism. Eleanor Roosevelt for instance, only properly entered politics – and even then only as a politician's wife – after having discovered her husband's affair with her own secretary, Lucy Mercer. Outliving her husband, FDR, she would help to propel the 1948 Universal Declaration of Human Rights in the historical world, a legal monument to hypocrisy and impotence. She had to sacrifice her own lesbian lovers to become political, even as her husband enjoyed his affairs as well as political power. Widely quoted for her snobby declamation that "Great minds discuss ideas; average minds discuss events; small minds discuss people", in this world she actually finds that she quite enjoys discussing people too. In an environment of growing sexual emancipation, Eleanor is able freely to pursue her homosexual passions, including with the renowned aviator Amelia Earhart. Eleanor learns to fly in this world after having divorced Franklin, who disapproved of having a pilot for a wife.

Divorcing the haughty American patrician is no bother under new socialist laws, and in this world Eleanor need not give any thought to the outdated social mores of the New England elite from which she came. On top of all that, with socialism in the US, the world has no need of empty statements of global rights designed to assuage bourgeois guilt. The newly single Franklin, never becoming a major public figure – let alone a four-term president – whiles away his time making cocktails for his party guests, at gatherings where they all fondly reminisce about the glory days when servants were less expensive and Negroes knew their place.

Others may never have had the opportunity to develop political careers. Hitler was swept up in the turmoil of revolution and counter-revolution in German Europe, but as fascism is still born in this timeline, a mass movement never emerges for him to take control of and lead. He drifts away from politics back into the bohemian demi-monde from which he emerged, finding more time to indulge his other interests, such as experimenting with quack medicines and shooting up speed. Some of his other interests – such as his incestuous passion for his niece and his coprophilia – raise eyebrows even within the libertine circles of frustrated petty artists in which he moves. Never propelled into positions of power, in this world a whole caste of fascist leaders never have the opportunity to indulge their reactionary views. Herman Goering, Hitler's air force chief in the historical world, devotes himself to alpinism and aeroplane stunts – thrill-seeking that eventually collapses into decadent opiate addiction to which Goering succumbed to in the historical world, too. Reinhard Heydrich, the single person with the most direct responsibility for implementing the Nazis' Final Solution, becomes an adept mid-ranking administrator in a middling industrial concern following his rehabilitation as an ex-*Freikorps* subversive during the Revolution. A committed racist at odds with the new socialist Germany, considered sinister and aloof by his colleagues, his career weighed down by his dubious political past, Heydrich remains an introverted, self-loathing loner who occupies himself with a string of affairs and his passion for music. In the historical world, Heydrich would be assassinated by a Czechoslovak special forces unit while acting as Hitler's viceroy in occupied Prague.

De Gaulle, whose legacy of authoritarian presidentialism and force-de-frappe *folie de grandeur* would shackle France well into our century, not only does not have a political career in this timeline, his life is also shorter. Stationed with French forces in the closing days of the GDR, De Gaulle's final hours are spent witnessing the Red Army put into practice a doctrine of fast-moving tank warfare that he had sought in vain to foist on the French army. The histrionic De Gaulle achieves his apotheosis leading a final charge on horseback against Red Panzers, realizing that the Russian Red Marshal, Tukhachevsky, leading the German Panzers is a more able theorist and practitioner of tank warfare than De Gaulle could ever had hoped to be. In the historical world the brilliant and ruthless Tukhachevsky would be tortured and killed on Stalin's orders. Tukhachevsky's murder and that of his peers in the Soviet military during Stalin's purges contributed significantly to the disastrous failures of the Soviet army in the early days of the 1941 Nazi invasion.

Ni Roi Ni Dieu

In this better world, monarchy would be ended everywhere by the 1950s at the latest. Depending on the fortunes of the Russian civil war, the Romanov children might have survived if not the Tsar and Tsarina, as the Bolsheviks initially intended a trial for Nicholas the Bloody. On the other hand, the family was shot in the early phase of the civil war when the city in which they were detained was on the brink of falling to counter-revolutionary forces. Thus they might have perished in their entirety in this world too. Elsewhere, where civil wars are less desperate and the revolution has irreversible momentum, or where monarchical prerogatives are already restrained by bourgeois political institutions, revolutionary vengeance would in all likelihood be less necessitous, less fierce and – in ex-constitutional states at least – political blame targeted away from monarchs. What is certain is that whatever the individual fortunes of this global caste of inbreds, monarchy as a political institution would be speedily euthanized and prevented from emerging elsewhere. The mass expropriation of religious endowments and lands, as well as the melting down and seizure of treasure contained in historic temples, monasteries, churches and mosques will provide a shot in the arm to the project of socialist modernization the world over.

Thus lamas, emperors, chiefs, princes, emirs, queens, bishops, dukes, counts, margraves, pashas, kings, maharajas, nobles, barons – all the dirt-encrusted golden filigree of thousands of years of hierarchy and oppression – are picked out and scraped off the surface of human civilization. In this world, the famous carnivalesque scene from Voltaire's *Candide* in which six dethroned monarchs find themselves at the same table in a humble inn, is repeated many, many times over and for real in those cities of the world that languish in the interstices of the great new global socialist federations: Tangiers, Cairo, Beirut, Tehran, Bangkok, Addis Ababa, Istanbul. These great cities of the developing world now benefit from the influx of refugees selling off their purloined jewels, furniture, heirlooms and furs. The European quarters of these cities are populated by a louche, impoverished caste of alcoholic White generals, aristocratic bar-flies, royal drug addicts, and a wider cast of intriguers, pretentious artists and decadent poets with a menagerie of illegitimate children, personal servants and hangers-on, imagining paranoid conspiracies of leather-clad revolutionary agents hunting them down long after they pose any political challenge to the new socialist states.

Some good novels emerge from this degenerate scene, otherwise the names of many ancient dynasties and houses disappear into the alleyways of these cities, forever forgotten. In our world, by contrast, the last nest of monarchical absolutism – the Middle East – is the direct result of post-war imperial policies that elevated tribal strongmen into leaders of nations whose borders were drawn up in British colonial offices and French palaces. Such arrangements would never have emerged nor endured had the revolution succeeded in Europe. Elsewhere it was only in 2006 that the quasi-divine monarchy of Nepal was replaced by a constitutional republic as a result of a revolution led by Maoist peasants. On this score at least, backwards Nepal is ahead of advanced Europe, which remains riddled with monarchs. Even if most of these are deprived of formal political power as individuals, they nonetheless still empower executives with their constitutional prerogatives while providing gimcrack ornamentation and Eurotrash celebrity distractions for the greying populations of sclerotic welfare states.

Arts and Letters

As with so much else in this timeline, the absence of Stalinism and fascism allows for a flowering of music, literature and culture not only because so many people live longer, but also because they live freer. In both the historical world and this one, the Russian Revolution would be associated with a tremendous sunburst of artistic innovation and creativity across countless domains – plays, cinema, architecture, music, art. The European and American Revolutions will be even greater: futurism, cubism, surrealism, atonal music will all flourish, collapsing neither into the decadence of conceptual art nor socialist realism, exploding into new art forms beyond our limited imaginations. Shostakovitch remains the premier composer of post-revolutionary Russia, and his work is freer to grow more abstract without being confined by Stalinist strictures. Mikhail Bulgakov's satires of socialist Russia are enjoyed across Europe soon after publication despite drawing the public scorn of Russia's new rulers, who are still sniffy about their backwardness and embarrassed by their reliance on bureaucracy to modernize their vast rural domain. The rapid decompression of the Russian regime in the face of European revolution means that the lives of artistic dissidents such as Anna Akhmatova will be that much better, sooner.

The success of the revolution in the Americas means that in this timeline Russia keeps her greatest science fiction writer, Isaak Osimov, better known to us as Isaac Asimov. Despite being born into an orthodox Jewish family, the talented and precocious Osimov's childish imagination is stimulated by watching a wave of socialist modernization sweep across the Russian steppe with the arrival of German technicians, agricultural specialists and engineers helping to roll out rural electrification even to the shtetls once scorned and persecuted by the Tsars. The arrival of these brilliant outsiders from a distant, super-technological future stimulates a torrent of science fiction stories from the grown-up Osimov about fantastic technologies and the human encounter with advanced alien civilizations. His books on human-robot cooperation in a distant future help to accustom his readers and the wider culture to a future of socialist cooperation that goes beyond the merely human.

Osimov's robot stories are inspired by the work of the Czech author Karel Čapek, whose 1921 play *Rossum's Universal Robots* introduces the world to this neologism for artificially manufactured servants, its etymological inspiration taken from the Slavic word for forced work(er). In Čapek's story the robots revolt against their redundant masters, massacring all humans except for Alquist, the only human left who still works with his hands – like the robots themselves. Given that the play is about a revolt by bio-androids that were built to free humans from toil, Čapek's work is widely celebrated – much to the anti-socialist Čapek's chagrin – as a utopian, futuristic fable about the workers' successful revolts against their capitalist masters in the twentieth century.

In the historical world, Čapek's play is seen as a dystopian warning, one of the many that keys into a deep and abiding fear in the modern imagination that our own creations might revolt against us. It is a tale repeated from Mary Shelley's *Frankenstein* through films like the *Terminator*, *Matrix* and *Blade Runner* series. They key into a basic suspicion about modern society – that it is organized in such a way that is beyond human control and purpose, in which things have displaced people. They tell us more about our own societies than they do about any possible future: we genuinely do live in a society in which we are overwhelmed by our own creations as a result of market organization. Čapek's play keyed into fears about people becoming or being machines as a result of industrial slavery. Thus Čapek's play is also clearly about the revolt of the workers, whereas today's modern fables on this theme reflect less the potential for workers' revolution so much as the redundancy of people in general. Our contemporary fables reflect a world in which the role of capital, machinery and technology is that much greater, the role of human labour correspondingly diminished. The autonomy and preponderance of capital under capitalist social relations haunts us. The absurd *Matrix*-style philosophical theories that we actually live in a virtual reality simulation constructed by advanced machine intelligences only reflects the fragmented consciousness and generalized lack of control experienced by the alienated individual of today. Why bother speculating that reality might not be real, once we comprehend the lack of social control that we really endure under actually existing capitalism?

Back to our better twentieth century. On the sharp edge of modernization, backwards Russia is highly attuned to science fiction, and Osimov and his followers will provide a set of cultural concepts for the majority of the world that will experience the adrenaline infusion of rapid socialist modernization and industrialization. Following the industrialization of Africa across the 1940—1950s, Afrofuturism arrives decades earlier in this timeline. With equatorial Africa providing the most geographically well-placed contiguous landmass for rocket launches during the last third of the twentieth century, a wave of cultural Afrofuturism in film and novels follows, as space ports and star cities spring up in the wake of the hydroelectric dams, power stations, roads, bridges and canals that now girdle central Africa from the Atlantic to the Indian Ocean. Despite an earlier boom in science fiction in this timeline, as the future arrives with the restructuring of political institutions and economic relations rather than just shiny new gizmos, the cultural and social need for science fiction also fades.

In the historical world of our late 1970s, the Scottish author Iain M. Banks would devise a tableau to host a range of science fiction stories – a distant communist future of such spectacular technological prowess and material abundance that has so far transcended violence, states and markets that the only way he could generate interesting plotlines was in discussing where this future humanity called "the Culture" intersected with less advanced alien civilizations, and the efforts to manipulate the progress of lesser alien species to more advanced, Culture-like levels. With his Culture overseen by artificial intelligences of superhuman capabilities Banks' portrayal is more that of a super-advanced benevolent welfare state engaged in humanitarian intervention with lesser societies than it is a communist vision. As communism begins to develop in this timeline by the 1970s, fortunately it has little in common with the lotus-eating vision of Banks' imagined Culture.

Some modern communists have also sought to get away from the hair-shirt and smoke-stack image of twentieth-century communism, campily chattering away about "fully automated luxury communism" on social media. Yet fully automated luxury communism – or #FALC on social media – does not meld particularly well with Marx's vision of communism. More the ideology of the hipster classes than Marx, FALC is the future as dreamt of by under-employed, work-shy graduate students who imagine that all of life could be spent battering away on a laptop in an over-priced café in east London, arguing about post-structuralist theories of identity on social media. Certainly in the timeline described here, accelerating productivity and massive investments in education would permit the cultivation of greater leisure time. The society that results would see more time devoted to sports, arts, entertainment, consumption, and so on.

Yet Marx's vision of communism was less about substituting genteel indolence for labour so much as exploding the two interdependent categories of labour and leisure, with their fragments to be reconstituted on a higher plane of social advancement. Individual pursuits would no longer be structured by public and private distinctions as work and hobbies, or restricted by formally articulated divisions of labour. Hence Marx's fondness for artistry as the appropriate model of work for a future society. That is to say, work conceived neither as labouring under the domination of a superior, nor as a social order of mass dilettantism, but rather as a model of passionate and meaningful individual pursuits liberated from necessity: "from each according to their ability, to each according to their need". For those more adventurous souls looking to test themselves instead of pursuing sensuality and hedonism, space colonization and exploring an increasingly industrialized, urbanized and therefore green planet will provide enough existential confrontation and terrors for any human being.

Back to our counter-factual history. Unlike Ozimov, other Russians do not fare so well. Alisa Rosenbaum flees post-revolutionary Russia to arrive in the revolutionary US in the late 1920s. The petty-bourgeois Rosenbaum despairs of the mass upheaval and popular enthusiasm that she sees there, anguished to see her social inferiors newly elevated, and the masses belatedly revenging themselves on the oligarchs of the Gilded Age. She is particularly heartbroken to see how the architects whose skyscrapers she so admires are drawn to the new artistic creativity and design possibilities unleashed by the revolution, not to mention the massive investments in public infrastructure commissioned by the revolutionary government. She falls into writing screeds dubbed "capitalist realism". Mediocre novels about square-jawed, steely-eyed entrepreneurs who rape women when they are not raping the economy, her books seem as bizarre and crude to her contemporaries as socialist realism does to us, as if cast adrift from a 1950s time warp in which the US was a grey, depressed and conservative society paranoid about foreign infiltration and political subversion.

Taking the *nom de plume* Ayn Rand, her attempts at political intervention in post-revolutionary public life with polemics entitled *Capitalism: The Unknown Ideal* are met with general merriment and derision. Hasn't capitalism had long enough to prove itself over 500 years that it doesn't work? How much more suffering must humanity endure at the altar of a failed ideal, based on brutalising and exploiting so many? Given the economic successes of the US revolution compared to the boom-and-bust cycle of pre-revolutionary US capitalism, her claims that capitalism has simply not been properly implemented fail to convince. Her libertarianism falls flat in the face of the civic, racial and political emancipation enacted by the Revolution. Depressed by her lack of public success, too domineering to cultivate a satisfying private life, Rand marries an alcoholic loser, whom she then bullies into letting her have affairs with her younger male followers. Her middle-class acolytes gather in various grouposcules that fission and denounce each other for heretical deviation from the path of Randist orthodoxy. Some of her followers set up capitalist utopian colonies in remote areas of the American Mid-West. These efforts are as successful and enduring as the libertarian hippy communes that we saw in the 1960s in our timeline, except the Randite colonies suffer for lack of women, who generally remain unmoved by the appeals of virginal libertarians dreaming of rape in Colorado. In short, Rand's counter factual biography is much the same in this timeline as in the actual historical world, except that in our world her writings are more successful, our more primitive intellectual life providing more fertile ground for her uber-mensch fables.

The other teenagers' philosopher whose life turns out differently in this world is Albert Camus. As the centrifugal forces of revolutionary nationalism are sublimated in this world into a new global order of transnational socialist federations, the French colonist Camus never descends into an apologia for French imperialism in Algeria, as he did in our timeline. Nor does his philosophy of the absurd or his novels about alienated losers strike a chord, not even among hormonal adolescent boys, Camus' most loyal followers in our timeline. Camus' ideas find little traction in a social and political world becoming more rational and dependent on direct human will, less subject to the forces of irrational spontaneity embodied in the market. Similarly, Jean-Paul Sartre's broodings develop some new insights into the philosophy of human freedom, although the absence of a Nazi occupation of France takes the piquancy out of existentialist agonising over human choice. As post-modernism never emerges, Paris will never become the capital city of irrationalism as it did in our twentieth century. Many aspirant French intellectuals will find themselves at a loose end while puffing away their lives on the Left Bank, as the consolations of philosophy are no longer needed.

Revolution in Europe will alter the life courses of Germany's intellectuals, too. Never forced to flee Nazi Germany as a Jewish radical, in this timeline Hannah Arendt remains in revolutionary Germany, with the result that she is even more under the thumb of her great tutor and lover, Martin Heidegger, who taught the teenage Arendt at the University of Freiburg. More an adept and insightful essayist than a truly original thinker, in our timeline Arendt would be elevated to become perhaps the world's premier philosophical Cold Warrior. Conveniently sidelining all the industrialists who bank-rolled fascism, she argued that fascism had more in common with communism than capitalism, as both were "totalitarian". She waxed nostalgic over the slave societies of ancient Greece, when politics was all about pontificating in the agora and never needed to address such trivial issues as the nature of work or material improvement in people's lives. Conveniently, given the Cold War, she also came to prefer the more genteel, slave-owning revolutionaries of the American Revolution over the passionate egalitarians of the French.

After the Second World War, Arendt would coach the sinister Heidegger on what to say to the Allies' de-Nazification panels, allowing him to keep his job – despite the fact that he had been an enthusiastic member of Hitler's party and at the forefront of rolling out anti-Semitism in the German academy. Many of

Arendt's core ideas were purloined from Heidegger's romantic anti-modern philosophy. Through Arendt, Heidegger's hatred of modernity helped to affirm Western liberals in their belief that mass democracy, political passion and engagement inevitably leads to concentration camps. In the timeline described in this book, following the Spartacists' Revolution in Germany Arendt remains much as she was in the historical world: a minor – albeit prolific – post-Heideggerian philosopher. Without any Cold War to fight, she never achieves any great renown and she remains a German rather than an American Heideggerian, spending too much time pining for her married lover rather than in coming up with her own ideas.

As fascism is stillborn, Heidegger is never given the opportunity to disgrace himself by lining up with Hitler. His philosophical conclusion that the best response to industrial society is to live in twee cottages in the *Schwarzwald* has little appeal, even among his most devoted students. Theodor Adorno is another character whose life is different and yet the same. A hate figure for the Alt Right today, the obscure Adorno's fragmented, gnomic teachings are credited for spreading the "cultural Marxism" that has ruined Western civilization and universities, overlooking the fact that students would need to understand his writings before they could have any effect. Adorno too was suspicious of modern society, variously fretting about such threats as jazz music, the invention of popular radio, and how man's domination of nature might backfire. Broadly sympathetic to the revolution, he nonetheless dislikes all its tumult and demotic energy, venting his frustrations in thin-lipped critiques of music theory as he watches the Revolution globalize the benefits of Western civilization around the world. The world will be spared the ruminations of Critical Theory.

As fascism and Stalinism contributed to dislodging Paris, Berlin, Moscow and Vienna as global cultural capitals in favour of New York and Los Angeles, so in this world Europe's lead is prolonged. The Hollywood film industry never benefits from the influx of brilliant cinematographers, directors and scriptwriters fleeing the European dark age of the inter-war period as in our world. The film studios of London and Berlin remain innovative, prolific, hypnotic and powerful, benefitting from political favour for radical new technologies and art forms and mass enthusiastic audiences. Global competition between the great film studios spirals upwards into ever greater bursts of creativity.

The development of music and culture will be dramatically different in this better world: technological innovations will allow for larger audiences and similar experimentations in form and style that we saw in our own world. The demotic and emancipatory cast of the revolution will propel experimentation and innovations that will uplift and transform various traditional and folk styles and classical music without sliding into pop music. In the timeline described here, the political success of the masses obviates the need for their cultural accommodation and the corresponding cultural dilution and decline seen in the post-war consumer societies that began emerging in the West by the 1960s. Ironically, the defeat of the proletariat in the historical world created the proletarian century – a century in which the working classes were variously flattered, praised, culturally elevated and condescended to across East and West – but a world in which they never ruled. Having failed to abolish class, the working class recreated itself, in a range of political compromises and accommodations built into the welfare state, and a range of demotic innovations that would begin the process of dissolving the achievements of "high culture" into the popular culture of the post-war period.

Sciences: Natural and Human

As revolutionary war recedes and reconstruction begins, science will benefit tremendously, while also remaining more evenly distributed around the world's advanced economies and major capital cities. Scientists are not scattered, exiled and murdered as a result of fascism, war and occupation as in the historical world. Perhaps even more importantly, the engine of science will not be war and geopolitical rivalry, and it will not be fragmented by jealous and secretive states. As borders, passports, spy agencies, arms races, state secrets and military spending decline in significance, science benefits from the socialist internationalism that facilitates wide dissemination of findings and theories through rotating academic congresses and international publication of leading journals. Young researchers and graduate students are freer to travel and work at the best research institutes, which in turn benefit from massive investments in R&D and education from modernizing socialist governments. As a result, science initially remains more German and breakthroughs in atomic physics and nuclear power take place throughout Europe rather than at the University of Chicago. The first functioning atomic reactor is built in Berlin, a compromise location chosen between the great physics institutes distributed around the continent. Budapest, Copenhagen, Berlin, Cambridge – all these centres of learning retain a prominence that they would lose in the historic world to Russian and particularly US universities when it came to physics. Without war and empire to inhibit access to global supplies of uranium and graphite, and boosted by the massive economies of scale possible in socialist planning, nuclear power will help to rapidly electrify continents across the 1940s.

It is space science and the rocket industry that perhaps benefits the most in our better world, as it will never be tainted by geopolitical rivalry and nationalist militarism. Nor will it be limited by the low horizons of profit, space tourism for the rich or the megalomania of Californian oligarchs. Outer space becomes the quintessential industry of the new order, pumped by human imagination and resources on a scale beyond the capacity of the market to deliver. With Germany and Russia unified in a socialist federation, and with both already being comparatively advanced in the science of rocketry, this facilitates in our better world the advancement of rocketry in leaps and bounds. The first person in space is a woman cosmonaut, Sarah Grynberg, chosen not only for her proficiency, aptitude and physical resilience, but also for what she represents – part Polish, part German, part Jewish and fully proletarian, she is a beneficiary of the social mobility and educational advance of the Revolution. Like Valentina Tereshkova, the first woman in space in our timeline, Grynberg is a cotton mill worker, whose peripatetic upbringing around eastern and central Europe make her an ideal candidate to represent humanity's advance on the stars. Following Grynberg, colonists begin arriving on Mars, the second red planet in the solar system, by the late 1960s.

When physicists realize the awesome destructive potential of nuclear power, they are grateful that the world is escaping the geopolitical and imperial rivalry of the past. Kiloton yields never enter the common vocabulary of nuclear scientists: it is something for passing moments of morbid speculation and shudders of horror before moving onto more pressing and interesting matters. Planck, Einstein, Bohr, Fermi, Heisenberg, Schrödinger are never torn apart by war and exile. Most physicists and scientists of this period are staunchly left-wing – a political stance that would cost them in the McCarthyite America of the 1950s. In this timeline, they are happy to put their shoulders to the wheel of the new revolutionary states, seeing the advance of science in the collective effort to slough off the irrational archaisms of religion, repression, states and markets.

The evolutionary life-scientists of this period in particular are magnetically drawn to Marxism: J.B.S. Haldane, Joseph Needham, C.H. Waddington and J.D. Bernal, whose collaborators Crick and Franklin would go on to discover DNA both in this timeline and in ours. Engels Institutes are established across a swathe of northern universities in England's industrial towns. These chemical, engineering and biology institutes are named for

Marx's collaborator and adoptive Mancunian, who took a passionate and abiding interest in natural science. His appreciation of dialectics in theorising human origins spurs insights that propel key breakthroughs in understanding human evolution. J.D. Bernal in particular saw Lenin, Freud and crystallography as the drivers of twentieth-century emancipation. In our historic world, the collaborative networks and institution-building that he pioneered found their fruition in CERN, the European organization for nuclear research, and the scientific citations index. In the historical world, Bernal's reputation would be shattered by his foolish defence of the Soviet charlatan-geneticist Lysenko. Lysenkoism would deal a blow to the development of Russian agronomy and biology from which it would never fully recovery, as well as dragging down Bernal's reputation with it. In the timeline described here, Bernal is spared this self-induced disgrace as Lysenkoism is never able to establish a grip.

The synthetic and totalising character of Marxism reinforces the intellectual breadth of these red scientists, who have tremendous intellectual range and organizational capacities. This helps in fostering discipline-building endeavours as well as avoiding the positivistic barriers between humanities, human sciences and natural science: Bernal had interests in Iranian art, Haldane in comparative religion, Waddington in Gnosticism and Needham remains in both timelines one of the greatest Western experts on the development of Chinese civilization. Europe's intellectual and scientific lead is prolonged in this revolutionary timeline, but cannot be prolonged indefinitely in face of the sheer scale and rapidity of industrialization and economic growth in America, China and Russia that powers further dramatic new breakthroughs on all fronts, and whose achievements would surpass whatever optimistic counter-factuals we might generate about the 1920s, 30s and 40s. Science itself will pass into something greater as society advances, perhaps coming to resemble that more holistic system of thought from the past, the natural philosophy from which science itself originally emerged.

While Marxism may help intellectually stimulate broad-minded scientists, another benefit of the revolution will be that it will be the end of Marxism. For what need is there for the critique of capitalism as capitalism recedes into the past? Marx's comments as regards the capitalist-infused character of his vision of communism are taken to heart by the Marxist leaders of new socialist governments, but are in any case implicit in the very functioning of technologically advanced, industrial societies rich in capital. A more orderly and rational world is a world with fewer paradoxes: Marx matters a lot less to a society that is surpassing capitalism. As society evolves past capitalism, Marx's science falls away, becoming the redundant ideology of a more primitive past, necessary to push humanity forward, but incapable of saying much about a society that is increasingly subject to conscious human purpose. Socialism finally liberates humanity from Marxism.

Epilogue: Reflections on the Worst Possible World: Our World

Perhaps Marxism has contributed nothing to the sum total of human development and freedom except to pile misery on misery in the form of catastrophic convulsion, subverting and mangling the gentle story of nineteenth-century human improvement. What state claiming to be communist could legitimately be held up as a model, except of authoritarian modernization and growth? If communism could simply be subtracted from the human story, many, many millions would have lived; many millions more would have enjoyed better lives. The centenary of the Russian Revolution has seen many wish it away, as it is said to have inaugurated a century of violence, bloodshed, totalitarian police states.

There are those of course who have sought to go beyond such wistful retroactive hopes and have taken practical action in seeking to carve communism out of history, as seen in the death squads organized by Chinese nationalists, German and Spanish fascists, Indonesian and Guatemalan dictatorships. Indeed, the Nazis sought to go further still. Hitler's propaganda minister Joseph Goebbels proclaimed that the Nazi ascent to power in 1933 would erase 1789 from history – the year of the French revolution that ushered in political modernity with the banner of *liberté, égalité, fraternité*. To root out communism requires rooting out the deepest, most fulsome and humane aspirations of modernity itself.

The notion that communism came from without to subvert humanity as the malevolent demiurge of shiftless conspirators and fanatical ideologues is obviously a moral fable that cannot withstand any scientific scrutiny of historical change. To see communism as the theory that wrecked the twentieth century, and Marx as the malevolent genius behind it, would be to underestimate the forces of modern nationalism, imperial and geopolitical rivalry, religious revivalism and millenarianism and the fissiparous character of modern capitalist imperialism and responses to it, in the form of autarkic attempts to catch-up by developing states. Capitalist modernity has been wracked with contradictions that would bedevil the twentieth century – one need only look at the apocalyptic collapse of the Ottoman Empire, for example, across 1916–22, to see the shape of twentieth-century horrors without a communist in sight. To blame the violent convulsions of the twentieth century on Marx makes as much sense as blaming Jesus for the Crusades or enslavement of indigenous Americans, or indeed blaming the Prophet Muhammad for jihadi violence today. The point is that the great world-religions are so deeply entwined through the fabric of human development over the centuries that causally to attribute singular episodes of human suffering and violence to them is to verge on tautology. Certainly, the breadth and depth of communist influence in the twentieth century can only be grasped by comparison to that of the great world religions – a point that is frequently resisted by Marxists and stridently maintained by ex-Marxists with all the zealotry and bad faith of the lapsed believer.

To be sure, comparing Marxism as rival to the great world-religions was the favoured tactic of anti-communist Cold Warriors, both Christian and secular alike. Following a US theologian, US president Ronald Reagan not without some justice, described Marxism as the second oldest faith, whispered by the serpent in the Garden of Eden: "ye can be as gods ..." Liberal philosopher of science, Karl Popper, who constructed an entire philosophy of science in opposition to Marxism, castigated Marx's ideas as pseudoscientific, having more in common with the venerable tradition of millenarian eschatology than modern science. Marxism was as irrational, fanatical and blind as any medieval mystic entranced by the end of times and the possibility of human redemption through a final bloody apocalypse-cum-revolution.

The affinity between Marxism and religion is real in as much as communism is a necessary social product. Society by its nature is hierarchical, organized around division, domination, exclusion and inequality of wealth and power. Such modes of life generate their counterpoint in the poor and oppressed coming up with visions of equality, simplicity, harmony, unity, redistribution and abundance for all rather than the few. These ideas will last as long as society lasts, which is to say forever – until communism. Unsurprisingly, recurrent revolts across history against oppression and inequality have taken a religious form. Such perhaps is the communism of the Khajirites, early Christians, Franciscans, Diggers, Shakers and others. Marx was at least as much a critic as a champion of these efforts.

Indeed, Marx could be said to be the first modern critic of communism – that is to say, a critic from the left of the "equalitarianism" that emerged out of the French Revolution in the nineteenth century, or what Marx described as "actually existing communism as taught by Cabet, Dézamy, Weitling, etc." According to Marx, this "communism is itself only a special expression of the humanistic principle, an expression which is still infected by its antithesis – the private system."[1] For Marx communism had to mean more than merely the opposite of private property. More precisely, Marx saw that unique features of capitalism raised the possibility of escaping the dialectic of social conflict. Instead of merely counter-posing equality to inequality, collective to individual and so on, he determined that it would be possible to transcend such oppositions by transforming the self-consciousness of communist revolt:

we do not confront the world in a doctrinaire way with a new principle: Here is the truth, kneel down before it! We develop new principles for the world out of the world's own principles. We do not say to the world: Cease your struggles, they are foolish; we will give you the true slogan of struggle. We merely show the world what it is really fighting for, and consciousness is something that it *has to* acquire, even if it does not want to. The reform of consciousness consists *only* in making the world aware of its own consciousness, in awakening it out of its dream about itself, in *explaining* to it the meaning of its own actions.[2]

If we forget Marxism alongside actually existing socialism, we may be condemned to pathologically repeat communist revolt in historic cycles yet to come – but without the benefit of Marx's efforts to make such revolts self-conscious, aware of their own origins and conditions of possibility. Instead we will remain trapped in the historic pit of "asocial sociability".

The only conceivable way in which the twentieth century could have been worse would have been a nuclear war between the USA and USSR. Yet humanity would have survived even this, too – in all likelihood with its social structures and political authorities mostly intact, just as Japan, North Vietnam and Korea survived and successfully recovered from the most punishing and exterminatory bombardments in human history. Humanity survived the apocalyptic twentieth century. That much at least is hopeful. On the other hand, the fact that humanity can still survive such terrible catastrophes is a more appalling fate than even the most extreme scenarios of human extinction dreamt up by the most extreme doom mongers. For confronting the reality of survival necessitates taking responsibility for the future. Even more dangerously and daringly, it requires reckoning with the possibility of progress and flourishing rather than indulging cloying fantasies of self-immolation. So what might a radically better world look like?

Endnotes

Chapter 1

1. This sections riffs on the opening of Alastair MacIntyre's *After Virtue*, Duckworth, 2003. Macintyre in turn was said to be inspired by Walter M. Miller, Jr.'s 1959 dystopian fable, *A Canticle for Leibowitz*.

2. George Orwell, *Homage to Catalonia*, Penguin, 2000.

3. Perry Anderson, "Renewals", *New Left Review*, Jan—Feb 2000, 17

4. Karl Marx, *The Eighteenth Brumaire of Louis Bonaparte*, 1852. Available: https://www.marxists.org/archive/marx/works/1852/18th-brumaire/

5. Peter Baehr, *Caesar and the Fading of the Roman World: A Study in Republicanism and Caesarism*. Transaction Publishers, 1998, p. 161

6. Karl Marx and Fredrick Engels, *The Manifesto of the Communist Party* (1848). Available: https://www.marxists.org/archive/marx/works/1848/communist-manifesto/ch01.htm

7. Ibid.

8. Karl Marx and Friedrich Engels, Part I, *The German Ideology*, 1845. Available: https://www.marxists.org/archive/marx/works/1845/german-ideology/ch01a.htm

9. Rosa Luxembourg, *Speeches to the Stuttgart Congress*, 3 October, 1898. Available: https://www.marxists.org/archive/luxemburg/1898/10/04.htm

10. Evan Mawdsley, *Thunder in the East: The Nazi-Soviet War 1941—45*, Bloomsbury, 2015.

11. This point draws on points made by Prof Richard J Evans.

12. Franz Neumann, *Behemoth: The Structure and Practice of National Socialism 1933—1944*, Ivan Dee, 2009.

13. The key thinkers here are Franz Neumann, Otto Kirchheimer

and to a lesser extent, Theodor Adorno.

Chapter 2

1. Michio Kaku, "The Physics of Extraterrestrial Civilizations". Available: http://mkaku.org/home/articles/the-physics-of-extraterrestrial-civilizations/
2. Karl Marx, *Capital* vol III, Part IV. Available : https://www.marxists.org/archive/marx/works/1894-c3/ch47.htm
3. Karl Marx, *Capital* vol I, ch. 10. Available: https://www.marxists.org/archive/marx/works/1867-c1/ch10.htm
4. E.A. Preobrazhensky, *From N.E.P. to Socialism: A Glance into the Future of Russia and Europe*, New Park 1973 [1922], p. 116
5. AJP Taylor, *English History 1914—1945*, Oxford University Press, 1970, p.1
6. J.M. Keynes, *Economic Consequences of the Peace*, Part II. Available: http://www.econlib.org/library/YPDBooks/Keynes/kynsCP2.html
7. Manifesto of the International Socialist Congress at Basel, 1912. Available: https://www.marxists.org/history/international/social-democracy/1912/basel-manifesto.htm
8. Ibid.
9. Keynes, *Consequences of the Peace*
10. Engels, in V.I. Lenin, "Prophetic Words", 1918. Available: https://www.marxists.org/archive/lenin/works/1918/jun/29b.htm
11. I take this point from Chris Cutrone. See further his "1914 in the history of Marxism". Available: http://platypus1917.org/2014/05/06/1914-history-marxism/
12. Leon Trotsky, *History of the Russian Revolution* vol. iii., Sphere, 1967, p. 124
13. Ibid., p. 147
14. Ibid., pp.147-148
15. This is taken from Loren Goldner's account of Bordiga's thought, available here: "Communism is the material human

community – Amadeo Bordiga today". https://libcom
.org/library/communism-is-the-material-human-
community-amadeo-bordiga-today (accessed 7 February
2017).

16. Isaac Deutscher, "Lenin's Last Dilemma". Available: https://
www.marxists.org/history/etol/newspape/amersocialist/deut
scher02.htm

Chapter 3

1. These words are Churchill's, although they were not spoken
upon Mussolini's demise. See Clive Ponting, *Churchill*, BCA
(1994), p. 350.
2. Lenin excerpts this speech of Lloyd George's in his 1920
polemic, *Left-Wing Communism: An Infantile Disorder.*
Available: https://www.marxists.org/archive/lenin/works/19
20/lwc/ch09.htm
3. Subhas Chandra Bose, *Words of Freedom: Ideas of a Nation*,
Penguin, 2010, pp. 8-9.
4. Winston Churchill, "If Lee had not Won the Battle of
Gettysburg", in J.C. Squire (ed.), *If it had happened otherwise:
lapses into imaginary history* (Longman's, 1931).
5. Eric Hobsbawm, *The Age of Capital*, 1975, p.155
6. The quote is from Marx's *Grundrisse: Foundations of a Critique
of Political Economy*, Penguin, 1993, pp. 460-461.

Chapter 4

1. Richard Ned Lebow, *Archduke Franz Ferdinand Lives! A World
Without World War I*, Palgrave Macmillan 2014, p.5
2. Ibid.

Epilogue

1. Karl Marx, "Letter to Ruge", 1843. Available: https://www.
marxists.org/archive/marx/works/1843/letters/43_09.htm
2. Ibid.

Zero Books
CULTURE, SOCIETY & POLITICS

Contemporary culture has eliminated the concept and public figure of the intellectual. A cretinous anti-intellectualism presides, cheer-led by hacks in the pay of multinational corporations who reassure their bored readers that there is no need to rouse themselves from their stupor. Zer0 Books knows that another kind of discourse - intellectual without being academic, popular without being populist - is not only possible: it is already flourishing. Zer0 is convinced that in the unthinking, blandly consensual culture in which we live, critical and engaged theoretical reflection is more important than ever before.

If you have enjoyed this book, why not tell other readers by posting a review on your preferred book site. Recent bestsellers from Zero Books are:

In the Dust of This Planet
Horror of Philosophy vol. 1
Eugene Thacker
In the first of a series of three books on the Horror of Philosophy, *In the Dust of This Planet* offers the genre of horror as a way of thinking about the unthinkable.
Paperback: 978-1-84694-676-9 ebook: 978-1-78099-010-1

Capitalist Realism
Is there no alternative?
Mark Fisher
An analysis of the ways in which capitalism has presented itself as the only realistic political-economic system.
Paperback: 978-1-84694-317-1 ebook: 978-1-78099-734-6

Rebel Rebel
Chris O'Leary
David Bowie: every single song. Everything you want to know, everything you didn't know.
Paperback: 978-1-78099-244-0 ebook: 978-1-78099-713-1

Cartographies of the Absolute
Alberto Toscano, Jeff Kinkle
An aesthetics of the economy for the twenty-first century.
Paperback: 978-1-78099-275-4 ebook: 978-1-78279-973-3

Malign Velocities
Accelerationism and Capitalism
Benjamin Noys
Long listed for the Bread and Roses Prize 2015, *Malign Velocities* argues against the need for speed, tracking acceleration as the symptom of the on-going crises of capitalism.
Paperback: 978-1-78279-300-7 ebook: 978-1-78279-299-4

Meat Market
Female flesh under Capitalism
Laurie Penny
A feminist dissection of women's bodies as the fleshy fulcrum of capitalist cannibalism, whereby women are both consumers and consumed.
Paperback: 978-1-84694-521-2 ebook: 978-1-84694-782-7

Poor but Sexy
Culture Clashes in Europe East and West
Agata Pyzik
How the East stayed East and the West stayed West.
Paperback: 978-1-78099-394-2 ebook: 978-1-78099-395-9

Romeo and Juliet in Palestine
Teaching Under Occupation
Tom Sperlinger
Life in the West Bank, the nature of pedagogy and the role of a
university under occupation.
Paperback: 978-1-78279-637-4 ebook: 978-1-78279-636-7

Sweetening the Pill
or How we Got Hooked on Hormonal Birth Control
Holly Grigg-Spall
Has contraception liberated or oppressed women? *Sweetening*
the Pill breaks the silence on the dark side of hormonal
contraception.
Paperback: 978-1-78099-607-3 ebook: 978-1-78099-608-0

Why Are We The Good Guys?
Reclaiming your Mind from the Delusions of Propaganda
David Cromwell
A provocative challenge to the standard ideology that Western
power is a benevolent force in the world.
Paperback: 978-1-78099-365-2 ebook: 978-1-78099-366-9

Readers of ebooks can buy or view any of these bestsellers by
clicking on the live link in the title. Most titles are published in
paperback and as an ebook. Paperbacks are available in traditional
bookshops. Both print and ebook formats are available online.

Find more titles and sign up to our readers' newsletter at
http://www.johnhuntpublishing.com/culture-and-politics
Follow us on Facebook at https://www.facebook.com/ZeroBooks
and Twitter at https://twitter.com/Zer0Books